HOT
AND
COLD
Turkey

Marshall & Hazel Thompson

Trafford rev.   10/01/2015

 www.trafford.com

North America & international
toll-free: 1 888 232 4444 (USA & Canada)
fax: 812 355 4082

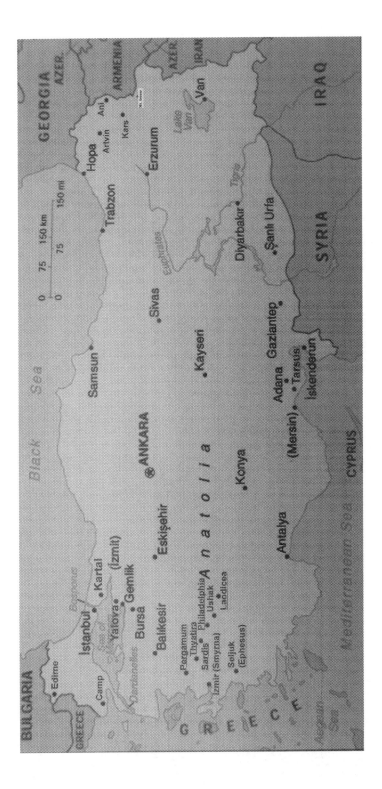

Contents

In the

Beginning

God

Created ...

Genesis 1:1a

FOREWORD

THIS BOOK WAS FIRST PUBLISHED in 2002 at the end of life changing history in Turkey. The two main contenders for the future, Great Road communism and Ataturk traditionalism, both lost to a gradual return to religious faith. The process shattered the famous Turkish "always united" concept cultivated from ancient times. A secular Turkey now exists along with the faithful. Where this takes them is a subject for future writers to record. This book concerns the agony of the process described and the planting of the Christian faith as a religious reality among the Turkish populations. The events recorded here are now part of the local history, but their effects will be felt forever.

So my word that goes out from my mouth; It will not return to me empty, but will accomplish what I desire and achieve the purpose for which I sent it.

Isaiah 55:11 Scriptures from New International Version

1

THE CALL ANSWERED

"WE CAN UNLOAD YOUR FURNITURE as soon as you pay the transport cost." But did I have the money? It was the end of a long summer of camps and trips. We stopped by Montreal in the summer for a week during the house hunting period and, of course, the payment of rent, deposit and other expenses foreseen and unforeseen. The Board would reimburse us, but we had to move in August into the apartment on Stanley Street three blocks from McGill University where we were to take courses in the Islamic Institute in September. We opened a bank account with our funds moved just before school started. The home office people were on vacation, a skeleton crew ran the business. Canadian summers are the crazy season; everyone is catching up on that annual pull of nature to the country. I had thought there was enough money to cover the additional expenses. The company unloaded our goods and we set up a rather minimal house. Ladies of Westmount Baptist Church—which we made our church home for that year, made a list of things that we needed and kindly lent us the missing items. This is not the first time we furnished our home with "Friendly Attic".

A Muslim student had formerly occupied the apartment and had the direction of Mecca clearly gouged into the floor. Hazel spent the year trying to get that bathtub clean. It looked like that whole surface had been chipped and ruined. The entire apartment had been painted, but this was just awful. Toward the end of the year, I, Hazel, finally got down to the real surface—and it was beautiful. Seems that with each painting, a lot of paint dripped into the tub and was never cleaned up.

Though most of the paint was white, there had been some pale pink; tan, blue, green, and then the accumulation of dirt between times had created that surface! If I had worked on it chipping it away or using a paint stripper, rather than using cleansing powders, or household cleaning fluids, I wouldn't have suffered so much with each soaky bath. Even Mr. Clean couldn't get it clean. There was no stopper, so I had to make shift until I found one to fit. Muslims prefer never to wash in still or stagnant water, they use the shower.

In September the expenses from moving came in the form of a cheque from our board and we took it immediately to the bank. When we talked to our teller she deposited the cheque and checked our accounts. "You were short on your moving cheque so we took the difference out of your savings account." She said. "We don't have a savings account." We said. "Yes." She said, "Hazel Thompson and here's your street number." "We live on Stanley Street, just above Sherbrooke here." The lady got a wide-eyed glassy stare and hurried off to consult others. The shortage was taken off our deposited cheque but no mention was ever made of a loan and I must suppose the lady never knew her funds had been borrowed to rescue a pair of ageing students following their God-given personal call.

The move was bizarre. Old veterans getting called to a new work with a new language to learn? The call had grown almost imperceptibly during the busy life of teaching in the high Andes Mountains. We were training our replacements in the work we were called to do there. Local people who were worthy and proven in the work that they were given were replacing gradually foreign staff. When we returned from home assignment to work in Bolivia, Marshall was prepared to write an end to our assignment there. He announced that the new term just starting would be our last in South America. In four years we would seek a transfer of our efforts to the Middle East. We started a church in the old city of Sucre and left it to the Bolivian Union to continue.

The Turkic people of Western and Central Asia are the last major people, numbering over eighty million, to receive the Gospel. I, Marshall, had done a research study of unevangelized fields for the home office and had statistics on outreach. Clearly the Turks were a neglected people. They needed friends and advocates in our increasingly difficult and hostile world. Few of them expected friends in the West.

We could be their friends for Jesus' sake. To be a friend one must show himself friendly. Literature and history of the Turks in the West is not written in a friendly manner. The Ottoman Empire was a source of fear and anger. They were in competition for land and empire. The outlook of grazers against the agriculturally based states was totally misunderstood or ignored. Westerners felt that states without agriculture or industry were barbaric and uncivilized. They were hordes; a word derived from the Turkish word for armies, "ordu": a disciplined mass of fighting men.

Some members of the Baptist council felt they were putting us in danger, sending us to an area where no evangelical churches existed to invite us into their country. But we pointed out that it was safer to be in God's will than living elsewhere out of his will. The situation was different than work in other areas because the definition of a Turk was to be a Muslim. All the Christians in their country were of another ethnic background with different languages and customs. They were considered competitors or aboriginals and potential enemies or allies of enemies. A Turkish Christian who would be loyal to his people and state was beyond their imagination. Such a thing did not exist. How would they receive such a reality? Could they live with it?

At the same time members of the finance committee stated that all our fields were responding well and that it would be a better investment of time and money to go to a more difficult field of work. Since there is no freedom of Gospel proclamation in Turkey we could only go in the capacity of friends who would provide what the national population was willing to receive from us. We knew they wanted to learn English; we would provide for their needs, we were teachers. It was one sure way to get visas and a welcome to their land. Both age and teachers are honored in their society and friends are everywhere welcomed. Our entry card had to be friendship. Teaching friends is always a pleasure and a good teacher will learn as much as the student; both being benefited in the process.

To be a friend required the sympathetic study of their life style, writing and music. We would make a formal start in the Institute of Islamic studies at McGill University in Montreal. Our subjects were Modern Turkish, Script and Phonetics of Arabic, The Tradition and Religion of Islam, and Marshall's auditing Hebrew. The social life in the institute was as important as the classes. We involved ourselves on the weekend in attending Westmont Baptist church and helping a Spanish congregation on Sherbrooke Avenue near the campus. It was the same year that Bill 101 made Quebec basically and legally a French-speaking province. We had good practice being the non-judgmental friend of all, and a peacemaker in spirit. Many great companies moved away, carrying all their goods and personnel. Campus life was a "Mardi Gras" of action and reaction with every opinion open to controversy.

At first they said in the registrar's office that we had to take a full course, then they decided we couldn't; we dropped two. But asked our teacher's permission to continue as auditors so we did. We worked very hard at all these, but the teacher of Arabic was very demanding, and the Turkish professor wasn't. Since we were planning to live in Turkey, when Hazel saw that the Turkish was losing out, we decided that we would have to drop out of Arabic in order to get what we really needed from our studies.

Westmount Church was an oasis where we refreshed ourselves on Sunday morning and Wednesday night. Mrs. Ellen Stevenson met us that first Sunday morning, saying she was sure I, Hazel, wouldn't want to be idle, and hired me on as a mission band helper. We also sang in the choir, and took part in that powerhouse of the church, the Wednesday evening prayer meeting.

Since the WMS met during the daytime, I was unable to take part in that. They still made a point of seeing that we had all our needs met though. Among the necessities of life they supplied were even a few houseplants! They were Hoya; in Spanish the letter J sounds like H; Joya means jewel. The blooms were scented broaches. So when classes were over, but before we left, I did get to one meeting, and I took all those houseplants with me. I said I couldn't leave them orphans, so would all who were interested, please take them home. The only thing that I asked was that they would pray for us each time they watered them. Years later, I would meet some lady who was still nursing one of those plants along, and still praying for us. One friend, each year, took slips from her plant and started them to sell at a fundraiser as the Missionary plant. She wrote a little jit that she attached to the plant; saying that the plant would flourish as you prayed for YOUR Christian worker each time you watered it! The idea of growth and gospel are a good match. The one promotes the other. At the end of the year we were prepared to leave for Istanbul. Pulling up roots is as hard for people as for plants, but it is the only way to get one in another spot where it can flourish and seed.

The Lord is with you...
Go in the strength you have...
I will be with you...
Judges 6: 12, 14, 16.

I will come and proclaim your mighty acts,
O Sovereign Lord;
I will proclaim your righteousness,
yours alone.
Psalm 71:16

2

FIRST DAYS

"Sorry, only the Post Office can sell the phone tokens. (*jetons*)"

One contact in Turkey had sent us a welcome and an invitation to stay at their house "while adjusting and getting things together." However, it was important that we call immediately upon arrival in Istanbul. We had been unable to contact them from Germany where we had stopped to interview a veteran of the work in Turkey. They did not know our arrival time and we did not know their address. We had enough of the language to count to a thousand and do greetings and key phrases in Turkish.

After clearing customs Hazel rushed over to get the *jetons* while Marshall changed money and defended the luggage from those who would thrust us into their friend's waiting taxi. His tension mounted as the airport shuttle prepared to leave for Taksim Square.

The post office attendant refused to sell one "*jeton*." He threw back his head and clicked his tongue in a negative while Hazel pushed the money forward and rephrased her plea. An official seeing her distress, explained in English that they only sold the tokens in quantity and gave her one. Then reconsidered and said "No, here take two!" We found mercy in the midst of stress, but we had to hurry onto the airport shuttle without phoning. We paid our fare and the bus fought its way to city center. We were lost in a city of seven million souls. We had two telephone numbers and the prayers of God's people, nothing more, with which to start our work. Standing at rush hour in the hub of the city, we wondered if it were enough.

The shuttle bus building was dark and dingy. Lines formed before the telephone stalls, although the attendants were trying to clear the building to close. Hazel dialed and a friendly voice in English reassured us. He said, "Just wait there. It will be at least 30 minutes before I can make it." We organized our luggage outside, and settled down in the chilly November night to wait. The taxies rolled by, pulled over and invited us to enter, while the traffic honked behind them. Forever later, Jay our new friend, parked at the curb and with a grin began to load the car. Exhausted, we drove away into the night.

Our friends did EVERYTHING to help us to get settled. They found we could study Turkish at the school where he taught English. They helped us get a post office box at the branch near the language school. Kay took us with her to the church where she attended with the children. They asked us to join them for Thanksgiving dinner along with 15 other friends. We became auntie and uncle to the children of whom we took charge. They hunted with us to find a place to live. They shared vital information about the people, city and the problems in church work. God gave us a family and ample work from our arrival. New friends made new possibilities.

We had gotten our basics very well, but we needed more language to converse and do research. Jay taught English and got a visa and a modest stipend at a Foundation with several hundred students above the age of twenty. Hazel maintained that, in order to attract potential teachers, they offered occasional Turkish courses and from these students who spoke English, recruited teachers for their English classes. We arrived on Monday, our hosts allowed us to get over our jet lag a wee bit, and on Thursday, Jay took Marshall to the language school. The administrator suggested we join a class of six that had started studying six weeks before. Marshall sat in on the class that day and decided he couldn't possibly catch up, and asked if we could begin another class and start from the beginning of their book which took quite a different approach than our Canadian classes. The administrator said it probably wouldn't work since they had to have five to start a class. Only one person had come asking to start from scratch, another had called, but it was economically impossible to start a course for beginners without a full quota, certainly not by Monday. Marshall told her we would pray about it. We did pray about it and went on Monday –and -- lo and behold, there were five of us. We bought our books and started with a wonderful teacher. She took us through the book of very basic lessons, and drilled us until we had perfect intonation. Both teacher and administrator became friends and spent time explaining things, even outside class.

They really wanted us to teach, and after Christmas, Hazel did take some classes and enjoyed the experience very much. Marshall, however spent his time in learning Turkish and researching for the historical novel he was planning to write.

Language experts insist that it is next to impossible to learn a foreign tongue after age 50, and Hazel gives her personal testimony that they are pretty nearly right. We were able to communicate, but never gained that proficiency that we had in Spanish. As a matter of fact, there are many Jews who live in Istanbul, descendants of those cast out of Spain by Ferdinand and Isabella. When we were buying in stores, and didn't know the word in Turkish, we reverted to Spanish, and were often able to make ourselves understood. That of course, led some people to believe that we were Jews! Marshall's goatee added to that impression. When Marshall felt "homesick" to hear Spanish, he would sometimes attend the synagogue services.

When the local Bible Societies Secretary heard that Marshall spoke Spanish, and could read some Hebrew, he gave him two copies of the Ladino New Testament, (of Spanish) written with Hebrew characters. Then, when Marshall needed a break from studying, he would read aloud from the book. Hazel suggested that he write it down in the Turkish Latin Alphabet, if he ever had the opportunity he could publish it for the local Jews to read. He did Matthew. However, terrorism and bombs in synagogue and businesses soon forced Jewish emigration to Israel and France. Many of the younger generation have forgotten spoken Spanish in Hebrew letters.

Another interesting development was reading the Shalom Newspaper- a local publication that wrote Ladino according to Turkish phonetics. "Que"= "ke", "hace"= "ase", "comunidad"= "comunitad", and sometimes it came out more like French "juventud"= "jeunesse". Actually, you heard many languages just walking down the streets of Istanbul. When we asked a young bank teller where he learned his English, he said he sold at the Grand Bazaar. And truly one young man selling there boasted that he also spoke Polish, Russian, Persian, Greek, Hungarian, Hebrew, Syrian and Armenian -- just enough to sell his wares.

English, German, and French were all taught in the 7th grade. You drew one foreign language in school and all your subjects were taught in the one language, which you drew in the lottery, if you chose to go to Secondary school. Arabic was added while we were there.

The Turkish people have a very high respect for teachers and age -- we were receivers of that respect on both counts. God had proven His ability to put us into a difficult situation and to make all things work for good. How long would we survive in this difficult near war setting? Could we learn the language? What would our help and testimony do for a people in desperate need of salvation? The only way to find out was to persist and keep trying. People will listen to friends who successfully suffer the same conditions as they. Our faith is tried by what we are called on to endure. Will it come forth as gold?

...the testing of your faith develops
perseverance.
James 1:3

3

BOOM!

"WELL, MARSHALL, THE REVOLUTION HAS come!" The explosion that had jolted us out of a sound sleep continued to reverberate. It was a BIG explosion. It had to be either a neighbor's gas bottle near by or an oil tank a long way off. It was our second morning in Istanbul, but dawn violence was not a new experience. We had spent a preceding 23 years in Bolivia, which had a history of 287 revolutions before our arrival. Though we had been there eight years before the first of six uprisings that we survived; some of the strikes we witnessed before then, had been as bloody. It seemed that the violence had just followed us.

We had to wait a while for the morning news, and of course, since it came on in Turkish, had to wait for translation. It seems that, eight kilometers away, at the confluence of the Golden Horn, the Straits of the Bosphorus and the Marmara Sea, a Greek tanker and a Romanian freighter had collided. The spark that ignited the crude oil in the tanker burned for a whole month, despite all the efforts of the harbor firefighters.

The initial blast shattered windows on both the European and the Asian sides of the Bosphorus, which is less than two kilometers. wide at the point of the encounter. The whole city was in panic. Traffic on the sea-lanes began to slow and since the ships are spaced only three minutes apart, it was backed up quite a way before alternate routes were determined and the flow was allowed to continue. Not only the traffic going between the Black Sea and the Mediterranean, but fishing craft, and ferries: large and small, plow through those waters.

The people in those boats: steam liners, fishing boats, and ferries; and the people in their cars, trucks and buses on the coastal roads and the Ataturk bridge; and the people in their apartment houses who were looking through their broken windows were all horrified at what they saw. Glaziers did a big business for several weeks. People on their way to work gaped as the column of smoke could be seen from any place in the city. From Taksim Square, the burning tanker itself could be seen, and crowds that had to change buses in the square jockeyed for the best vantage point to get a glimpse of it.

After a couple of days it was towed out of the shipping lanes, but was still visible from Taksim, and all the nearby coasts. Some people, who had no other reason that brought them to a viewing spot, took the family to one of the parks for a picnic, just to see it.

We moved after a few weeks, and relocated just about two kilometers from the wreck. One evening upon retiring, I saw through a tiny part in the curtains a bright orange light illuminate our patio. "Wake up, Marshall! Look!" I yelled. Subsequent flashes of light and the boom helped me... Boom... BOOM! that followed, and we rushed to the window. It looked like OUR patio was on fire, but we couldn't see the flames. A few minutes later, our landlady knocked on our door, and we trooped to the picture window at the other end of the apartment. We had been looking at the back garden, with the whole apartment building (6 stories high) between us and the burning tanker, and had still seen that startling brightness. From the front, the boat itself was visible. It had burned through the bulkheads to three more storage tanks, and so continued to explode and burn...it seemed as though all their efforts to extinguish the flames were in vain.

When a month had passed since the collision--it was now mid-December--the snow came. We were shopping for furniture for our new apartment, which was in the center of town, not far from the Hilton Hotel. The crude oil on the tanker began to chill, stiffen, and solidify, so that finally the flames flickered, were smothered by the snow and died. Our English-speaking neighbor stated: "I knew that the crews couldn't kill it, only God could put out that furnace."

We had been following a beacon of friendship. From Jay and Kay, to Gonul at language school, to our landlady who would open the way to other new friends.

As with the Israelites on the road to the Promised Land: so that fire served as our cloud of smoke by day and pillar of fire by night showing us God's presence with us in this new land. It had served as an introduction to the city of Istanbul: largest citadel of Islam in Europe and left a strange assurance that this was His purposeful leading - a signal of changes to come. "Tell the children of Israel to go forward."

We all look for signs of God's leading or approval of our ventures. We usually find some omen for or against some enterprise we cherish. Idolaters or believers, we long for and look for approval. But only the future can reveal if that sign and faith were true. There are ways that seem right to many, but the results lead to disaster and death. A faith that bears good fruit is the one sure sign of God's leading.

...seek and you will find...
Mathew 7:7

Marshall & Hazel Thompson

*I will lay down and sleep in peace, for you
alone, O Lord, make me dwell in safety.*
Psalm 4:8

4

HOME HUNT

IN A CITY WHERE A thousand persons arrive each week seeking housing and work, you would expect crowding. The city core was full of six to ten story buildings marching along every main street. Nestled among the hilly suburbs were ranks of townhouses with dainty little front and back gardens. Topping many hills, or beside the Bosphorus waters, were opulent mansions with acres of formal gardens, mirror pools, and high stone walls bristling broken glass bottles or lacy wrought iron fences crowned with spikes. Both walls and fences were for protection from thieves, but the walls kept out prying eyes as well. At the other end of the spectrum, where there were undeveloped pieces of land, *"gejecondos"* sprouted - ramshackled huts - put up in a night, made of flat beaten tin and cardboard. Living space was at a premium.

While other places in the world demanded 20% of your income for lodging: Istanbul renters paid 50% or more! It was one of the highest rates in the world. With galloping inflation - the longer you stayed and rented your apartment the better your price. That is: he started paying the equivalent of $160. After sixteen months, inflation had reduced the 9,000 TI to only $100.

Our host's home was enormous-- only six rooms, but big enough to divide so that it seemed to be ten ample rooms. We decided that two bedrooms would be enough for us (we did want a guest room) but we understood that we could expect to pay two or three times more than locals did. We talked about some of the things that we would need, and started looking.

Jay and Kay asked ALL their friends about prospects, looked in the newspapers, drove us up one street and down another looking for papered-over-windows, absence of curtains, FOR RENT signs, or any other indications that there was a vacancy. We rang doorbells, talked to *kapajis* (building custodians) checked community bulletin boards: and that is where we found our first room.

At our language school, a local member of the sponsoring association, who spoke English well, advertised a room. We had spent hours waiting for buses, riding on buses, getting lost by taking wrong buses; going to and from our friend's house. We were in luck; this room was only five short blocks from the language school.

Our landlady would serve us breakfast in our room, and there were restaurants nearby where we could get lunch and supper. The twin beds were pushed together to seem like a king-sized bed. An enormous wardrobe spanned one end of the room: one of the three sections was reserved for the owner's storage, but the other two held all our meager clothes. The window, which faced south and caught the weak rays of the wintry sun, reached most of the way across the back wall. It gave a delightful view of the gardens of the official residence of the mayor of Istanbul. The apartment was only on the second floor, but it had an elevator and central heating. There was a round table and two comfy chairs to serve as our breakfast nook and study area. The owner assured us that we would be welcome to join her in her living room for the news on TV each night. There were advantages for her as well, because it would give her the opportunity to practice her English every day. Counting from our arrival it took three weeks for us to find this place and move in. Our prayers were answered. It took three more weeks to find the apartment that we would occupy for the rest of that first visit to Istanbul.

Marshall once said that he would be willing to stay where we were if it wasn't for our meal situation. There seemed to be no middle ground between a grilled cheese sandwich and a "chateaubriand": quick lunch or formal dining; two dollars or fifteen. Breakfast, too, soon became a problem. We were paying by the week, hoping that we would find an apartment before the month was gone. The breakfast cost more than the landlady had figured on, so she put up the rent each week. She also cut the quality and quantity of the breakfast; finally stopping it altogether. We were driven to prayer again.

Several times our landlady argued for an increase for our breakfast cost and presented the facts forcefully. She was shocked when I, Marshall, agreed with her analysis and cheerfully agreed to pay more. She was not accustomed to men taking her word willingly.

We explained our food problem to our landlady, she suggested an alternative to eating out. Just a few blocks away lived a cook she knew. The lady cooked for ten families, sort of a boarding house" at home. The difference was she paid a little man to make the rounds delivering these meals to your house, on or about 12 noon; just after classes. It was enough to feed one meal to a family of five. She took us to visit the cook, and we decided to try her out. We tried to negotiate for a half portion, but she insisted she couldn't do that. There were two vegetables and meat each day, and desert every fourth day. Sunday she did not serve. We agreed on a starting date and promised to return to pay her. We would have a good diet.

About this same time our furnace broke down and our nice room was cold. The "*kapaji*" had been unable to get the recommended fuel oil and the owner had bought a heavier grade. Electric cuts had become a part of a rationing process for the city. The electric spark starter and fuel pump were off part time, and as the apartment block cooled, the oil chilled and thickened. The pump could not handle the heavy viscous oil and broke. Replacements were not available. Language school was our only warm refuge. We wore all our heaviest clothes. Everyone in the building suffered. We were obliged to pray for warmth.

There come moments of doubt and trials just when you think things have been resolved and there is smooth sailing ahead. It requires a renewal of prayer and faith at the moment when it seems that all has failed and come out badly. Don't give up, rather be glad, the moment of truth and proof has arrived. Christ will be glorified in you.

You need to persevere so that when you have done the will of God, you will receive what he has promised.
Hebrews 10:36

5

BEDLAM ON BUSES

CITY BUSES WERE PACKED TO the front door, yet a few more people would desperately place themselves in the doorway and push. The driver would try to close the door and usually it would stick because a body would block it and everyone would yell "you rue" meaning walk or move back. Like the light in the refrigerator, the bus would not move until the door was fully closed. Those in the aisle would strain toward the rear and those getting off two or three stops up the line would get up and start working toward the exits at the center and back of the bus. However, the order and discipline of the people was not lax. No fights broke out and sometimes gallantry was clearly displayed. Seats were given by preference of the one departing to the aged, the pregnant women and adults carrying children. We noticed a big sign at the front of the bus. It proclaimed:

> ### *PLEASE GIVE UP THE SEATS AT THE FRONT TO VETERANS AND THE ELDERLY.*

My white hair often netted me a seat—and if there was no man who would get up, often a young woman would offer me a place. One day when I had on a big sun hat, and my white hair couldn't be seen, I was embarrassed that a young man was nestling up close, improperly. I snatched off my hat and looked down my nose at him - making HIM the shamed one! The elderly, incidentally, were also allowed to exit through the front door. Others had to fight, wiggle, and ooze through to get out a side or back door. If you were getting off in two stops, you said,

"Thanks, but NO thanks!" if someone offered you a seat. You began to work your way through the crowd from the minute you stepped on the bus, so you could get off at your stop. There was never a "lull," though sometimes they ran the buses on certain lines a little less frequently. Unless, of course, there was a traffic jam, bomb or other disruption along the line. At nine PM a new, slower bus schedule began, that ran until one in the morning or curfew time, if it came earlier. Then there was a four hour pause until bus traffic began again. Then everyone had to use taxis or walk! At the peak rush hours, you might get on at a side or back door, and pass your ticket up to the driver, rather than risk getting stuck in the crush, and missing your stop. The people were quite used to passing up tickets and very honest about it.

Monthly passes were sold for a little less than what you would normally pay for 60 rides, and saved you a little. To get your pass the first time you had to take two pictures, fill out an application, and wait a couple of weeks until it was processed. Then you received a laminated card with a pocket. Each month you bought a small color-coded card to put into the pocket. Then you could use it on that bus line as many times as you wished. You just flashed it at the driver--no punching--so it was much more convenient. You might find that the shortest way from home to work was taking two or three buses, which wouldn't have been convenient if you were paying out a ticket, or had to get a transfer each time you changed. With a ticket you have to get on at the front door, and fight for a place. With a pass you got on the at the side door, showed your pass from there, and had no fight to get off five blocks down the road. When the ticket box became too stuffed, the bus driver dropped a match into the box and it burned up the tickets. It frightened me the first time I saw the driver do that. They had no way of knowing how many people rode the bus!

Since many buses made loops, it might be more convenient for you to take three other buses when on the way home. By knowing all these little short cuts a *"mavi cart"*(blue card) represented considerable savings in time AND money.

The bus stands, usually with a shelter from the winter rain or summer sun, were many blocks apart. The walk between the stops was considerable, but people would sometimes leave a crowded stop to walk to the stop before, along the route, in the hope of getting on. The "minibus", on the other hand, was paid according to the distance traveled and was quite convenient to use; once you got past the long line waiting to fill the next one. They unloaded near the dock or bus center and roared up to the line some blocks away to load about 15 people and start their round again. Their stop markers were usually about a half way between the bus stops. It was awkward to use both. But when buses were full and traffic heavy you would walk between stops and take whichever waiting line was shortest. There were lots more minibuses so they came much more often. They almost looked as though they were pushing each other along the road like a parade of circus elephants. The minibus gladly stopped when they had seats, even in traffic. If it was too crowded, and you chose not to get on; you saved him a stop by saying no. You said no by looking up at the sky and turning up your nose at them! In ordinary conversation, you also clicked your tongue, but from that distance they couldn't hear you.

They tell the story of one foreign girl asking in careful Turkish if this was the right bus to get to Topkapi. The bus driver responded with this turned up nose three times, and she still didn't understand his "no". So he got out of the driver's seat, took her by the shoulders, turned her around and gently started her down the steps.

Early Sunday morning was the only exception to this rule of congestion, everyone else slept late. After 11 o'clock the streets and buses filled with travelers because Sunday is family and sports day. Technically the country was 99% Muslim but only a minority were religious. It was Ataturk's decision to keep the universal day of rest. But the Sunday football game brought congestion worse than any workday.

The buses were filled with singing, shouting men, young or old, displaying their colors. Fights sometimes occurred when two antagonistic team fans occupied the same bus.

In one of my conversation classes with a group of Doctors, we were using our "Football vocabulary"(called Soccer, here). Immediately, the group split into the fans of Fenner Bache, and Galata Saray. One lady doctor told us how she avoided problems in her family. Seems her husband was a Fenner Bache fan, while her son favored Galata Saray. When she was asked, she answered that she was for Galata Bache.

Since these games were hotly contested, and the contest often continued past the closing gun: the police were out with riot squads at ready near the stadium. The women and children were usually visiting relatives, waiting for the men to return for the supper hour. Then, all would crowd the bus or minibus to go home. Women were always escorted at night and only men were out to curfew time. We often heard shooting after dark, when robbery and street graffiti-painting flourished.

We stayed our first three weeks in Etiler, a suburb north of the city. Levent was a nearby sector where the buses passed through or had a terminal. There were letters beside the numbers, which indicated variation of route and confusion of mind to those who had not grown up with the system. The route was called a "*hat*" in Turkish, but if you got on a bus with the wrong number or different letter you ended up having an adventure rather than arriving at a known destination.

"How many "*hat*'s" do you try before you find one that fits?" We had constant trouble getting the right buses and getting on through the press of anxious people waiting. Two or three buses might pull up to a downtown stop, and younger people would run to look at all the names; yelling or pointing to one for their friends to come if it was the right one, or shrugging in despair if it wasn't. Lines formed of those trying to force their way on. The drivers would try to close the door when maximum capacity was reached. Some would take a bus that paralleled their route; then get off and walk to another closer line where they could find a bus that would go to their destination. It looked like an irrational frenzy, but was really methodical madness and most would arrive tired, ruffled and rumpled to their home turf. What could you do about it? Most sighed and did the same thing every day.

The people on the buses were not friendly: considerate, yes, but no one smiled. Strangely, no one talked. No one read the newspaper. We wondered why and learned from our language teachers. Turkish was in a rapid state of language evolution and political change. In the 40 years since Ataturk had reformed the language to use the Latin alphabet instead of the Arabic one, they had moved linguistically more than we had in 400 years from "King James English" to the present.

By eliminating much Arabic, introducing archaic Turkish and new technological words, vocabularies expanded. Religious language is conservative and slow to change; while scientific language constantly needs new words. Many times they are just taken over from the language that made the new discovery. The secular Kemalist state was being pulled in two directions by the changing world. Leftists and rightists were killing each other and each had a newspaper that reflected his language and views. You could tell a man's politics by the newspaper he read and his spoken vocabulary. No one wanted to wear his political opinion on his sleeve where it might invite friction or damage. We learned very little vocabulary while riding to and from our destinations. The exception was the occasional young student learning English, who boldly tried to practice speaking it. Many times we ended up giving an impromptu English lesson on the bus or the ferry. An invitation to our home for tea was in order, or they would ask us to visit them. We made many friends that way.

Our relief was great when we moved to the center of town. We rapidly learned our city. We could and did walk almost everywhere: language school, church, bank, park, neighbors, and shopping. It was easier to keep warm on those dark November days walking than waiting for a bus.

On the way home from language school, we developed a web of friendly people: the kiosk where we bought our newspaper, the local grocery store for bread and other staples, the store where you always stepped in to warm up and admire their goods, and the man at the taxi stand across the street.

By moving to the center we gained health and reduced stress. After all, the bombing and shooting went on in the suburbs, too. Again, God had given us the better part. We became a drop-in center for young Christian summer workers. New friends that came from all over Europe. "All things' work together for good to those who are called according to his purpose."

The path of the righteous is like the first gleam of dawn, shining ever brighter till the full light of day.
Proverbs 4:18

6

FAST FOOD

EVERY LITTLE HOLE IN THE wall had some entrepreneur selling something on the main streets. In the residential areas, each six story (or more) apartment building had its own shop to accommodate the residents by selling bread, milk, ice cream, candy, the newspaper and other necessities. At movie theaters candy bars, Eskimo bars, and pop corn were available. Wherever lines formed or people waited there would be carts or stores to sell pickles (not vinegar-y but salty), sandwiches heated on a metal grill, or pizza to be microwaved. Booths under bridges or in subterranean passages offer the chance to have a bite of something nice. Often chairs and tables, even with umbrellas, clog the sidewalk nearby for your comfort. Some serve only one food--no need to order. You sit down and wait. Soon a bowl of "*humus*" (chick-pea meal) appears with a quarter loaf of bread on each end of an oblong platter and two quarters of tomatoes with parsley sprigs on top. The pale dish of pureed chick peas is decorated with a thin curl of spicy, hot vegetable oil making a red "C" in the middle. In other places soup is brought to you. Another makes only rice pudding. Whatever the specialty you get, you pay on entering, and receive a receipt. When your food has been delivered, the receipt is torn a little (so they know you have received your food). If you are really hungry, you state a number, to indicate you want more than one. Presto, here it comes, now you add the condiments and enjoy!

On warm days, and always available in the parks and near the stadiums where soccer matches were scheduled, another strange sight appeared: a handcart (the size of a kitchen table) with bicycle wheels, and a slight rim around it that held a bed of ice. On the ice sat long, plump cucumbers. When you bought yours, the vendor peels it; splits it twice from one end, leaving you with four pieces ending in a small part to serve as a handle and providing you with a welcome chilled treat. It was easy to eat, and no litter afterward!

In summer the vendors would bring out green fruit on ice. Each in its season. I mean really raw, under-ripened plums, almonds and hazel nuts. They were acid and the kind mother warned us against when young: but buy and consume them they did. In the evenings near the parks where people congregate to enjoy the new heat and pass time, small spits of roasting meat were offered.

Some men walked along with what looked like a ten ft. pink bottlebrush, on a Sunday in the park. These poles had a row of clips at hand-span intervals. Each clip held quite a large bag full of cotton candy. But food and drink were not the only offerings. Others had a similar arrangement that was covered with colourful balloons. On holidays, they walked down EVERY street, and people on the second floor could make their selection from the window or balcony of their apartments.

There were toys, jump ropes, and water pistols for sale at the entrance to the parks and museums, even in the city centre when it was warm. Young men in their twenties seeking work would stand all day selling wind-up cars, dancing dolls, animated balls and figures of all kinds. These childish trifles were offered at low prices, the commission might be enough for cigarettes or a lunch. There is little wonder that many become mercenaries hired to fight in Middle Eastern and African wars. Some were in construction crews that worked in oil rich countries. But most stayed close to home taking any kind of job to fill in their lives. Every train and ferry boat that moved in the city had its share of sales persons offering pens, pencils, paper, note books, in sets and all sizes and combinations for less than store prices to the students going home. Later men going home on commuter trains, would be offered small TV antennas, athletic socks and sheer nylons (for the wife); shaving kits, kitchenware or Korans and much more. They would walk into a different car at every stop and promote until they arrived at another station. Then slipping out they would do another car until the end of the line. With another ticket they repeated the itinerary and it made for good business and entertainment for the passengers. On one trip across Marshall watched as the man inserted a small cutting plastic spout into the end of a lemon. He poured out a tea glass of juice, as if it were a bottle. We were sure the seller had squeezed it some, but when I got it home and tried it out myself, it really worked. Sometimes a person would get on with a sad story of loss or illness and displaying an official letter, would beg aid from the charity of the travellers. They too seemed to do well. They called down blessings on everyone as they left to re-enter another car. The ships were worked in the same way from deck to deck; forward, aft and centre. This made for constant activity and even the lone traveller found interesting sights or even an economical purchase on his way home. They speak to each of us of the transitory nature of life and the presentation of new opportunities each day.

Friends share the disasters of the day or the clever bargains they made in great detail. Any purchase you make will always produce a story of how they managed to get a better product or the same for less. Gloomy faces were worn in public, sad stories of others tragedies were expected. They were always surprised by our laughter, smiles and stories, but they liked it. Friendship should be fun.

Life is full of unexpected turns and twists; nothing remains the same for long. God speaks of a coming world where the kind of changes we are accustomed to will not occur. No pain or crying. No feebleness or disease. No sin, gain or loss of goods, striving about goals and timetables. No need for material possessions or seeking of emotional satisfactions. Most of us are not prepared for a steady-state universe. Eternity is too different for us to desire it. Yet, we are all going there and had better find out something about our destination as we carry our portable pleasures with us. They, as well as we, may not all fit comfortably in the new future.

Hatred stirs up dissention,
But love covers over all wrongs.
Proverbs 10:12

7

DAILY DEATHS

THE TURKISH REPUBLIC IN 1980 was near to civil war and anarchy existed in both city and country. My body count from various media sources registered an admitted 30 victims each week. Name, age and vocation were treated in the obituary while party affiliation was not usually mentioned except in news write-ups or radio eulogies.

We heard the morning news on the radio, the 8:00PM news on TV with a neighbor (who filled in all the fine points that we missed in Turkish) and bought a newspaper on Saturday and studied it so we could answer questions about in a class on the following Monday. We had an English friend who had lived there many years and was a real scholar. He did translation for a living. He consented to help several of us newcomers with practical conversation classes and religious vocabulary. Our regular Turkish teacher was one of the best, she knew Standard English and even some English slang, but she just couldn't answer all our questions. Before we asked, our man knew what we wanted to know--since he had been down that road first.

The Saturday paper had a "FOTO ROMAN" (a movie in a comic book format; complete with balloons.) that he used as a basis for his classes. It had real live conversations: daily Turkish with all its slang. There were many things we DIDN'T need, like: "Cut him down." "Hands up!"; "Don't move or I'll take you apart!", in the action scripts. Romances too, were excessive, "Leave me alone!" "What a hunk!"; "Terrific!"; "Kiss me again".

Our written assignments, however, were to be translated from the front pages, always full of interesting disasters. People or governments were constantly under attack; accusations and fisticuffs were presented for daily scrutiny. Lots of people died in many places and in violent ways. Kidnappings were common.

Page two in the Monday paper was dedicated to just a resumé of the week before: athletic events, entertainment, new businesses, bankruptcies, explosions, bank robberies, fires, riots, and lists of the number killed in each city. Numerous other people were missing, no clues or facts reported, just gone. Had they eloped, evaded debts, fallen in the sea, been captured by the army, by the mafia, by the opposition, disciplined by their own death squads, or committed suicide? No one knew. A few unidentified bodies turned up, some of them showed signs of torture: cigarette burns or missing fingernails.

News in papers, television and radio inquired into the daily quota. They ran ads, notices and programs on both the dead and the missing.

> **"Disappeared in November.**
> **Please forward any information to..."**

Husbands, wives, children, parents and relatives searched for traces, pleaded for contacts, hoped for clues. They included photos of the beloved. Television ran pictures of captured guns. Those arrested were shown standing behind a table with an orderly display of illegal weapons, the party propaganda pamphlets, and at times even the typewriter used to write them. The subversive messages of alleged government crimes filled these crude brochures and indicated salvation's way via the outlawed party, "Dev Yol", the Great Road.

The effect of these scenes on the audience was mixed. While partisans cheered and opponents groaned, those caught between the extremes felt pity for the captured, whose faces were shown with the evidence. A few stared defiantly at the camera, while the majority hung their heads in shame trying to escape recognition. Some women cried. These showings concerned hidden weapons and messages found in homes, so the whole family might suffer for the actions of one or two. The jails were overflowing with detained people.

In times of fear it is of comfort to know people who can help you. The fact that our house was the property of a sergeant in the Turkish army was a source of comfort to us. He would come by in a jeep on some occasions to check on us and we would chat a while. His friendship enabled us to get the scarce propane gas tank we needed for cooking and heat. He bought us one from the Army store(with our money). We were the envy of some neighbors; we had an IN with the Sergeant.

However, it did get us a visit from the district communist leader to check us out and see what we were up to. He asked if, since I had money, would I give him my jacket? My answer was to feel the lapel of his overcoat and suggest that we make a trade. He left on that one and didn't appear again. I am sure that others reported our activities to him. Watching eyes are everywhere when life depends on staying aligned.

Actually, the Great Road was only one of many parties demanding various degrees of change. More than 40 years after his death, Ataturk was still the magnetic center of Turkish politics. Each party claimed itself as the true follower of his teachings in the logical progression toward his goals. Violence had accompanied the gaining of the republic: violence would again accomplish his purposes. The 'father of the Turks' knew best. Only the extreme religious right rejected this premise. But their religion's founder too, had chosen the way of war to bring about his aims and proclaim his message. The only man who encouraged and stimulated personal freedom under God to choose and not to be forced was the Rabbi Jesus, Yeshua in his own language, meaning Savior. He said: "You will know the truth and the truth will set you free." On other occasions he said "I have come as light into the world. Walk in the light while it is with you." To others he said, "Your faith has saved you." What does he say to us?

...let them come to me for refuge; let them make peace with me. Yes, let them make peace...
Isaiah 27:5

8

HOME RUNNING

WE COULD HAVE CAUGHT A plane home. We could have retreated to a hotel and made some expensive arrangement to stay there. We had arrived in a crowded city in a time of party strife and daily street violence. We wanted to move out of our formerly warm but now cold and lovely room to an apartment of our own. We had found an abundant supply of good food cooked in Turkish style, now we had to find a suitable place to live. We had looked for weeks - nothing.

As we returned to pay the cook we walked by a "FOR RENT" sign, and agreed to investigate on the way home. After concluding our business, we started back and noticed there was someone inside the apartment. The landlord noticed us and leaned out of the ground floor window and invited us inside the building. Then, after entering, our communication skills proved inadequate. We trooped over to find a neighbor who he knew could translate.

Reg, a British navy retiree and his Turkish wife Semiha lived just across the street. Their 19-year-old son Errol was being inducted into the army. The door was just around the corner. Semi took over the negotiations right away, and though there were quite a few words we recognized, she translated every once in a while to keep us in the conversation. She started by knocking the 11,000 TL(Turkish Lira) asking price down to 9,000 TL and he didn't object. When we revealed that we had brought NOTHING, had hoped for a "furnished apartment" and didn't want to spend a lot for our 18-month stay; the conversation took a different turn.

They, the owner (a sergeant in the military police, whom we called Sergeant for our whole stay) and Semi, began to tell us all the things they could get together for us to use. The sergeant's wife wanted a new dining room set, and would be happy to lend us her old one. They had two carpets that would cover the badly scarred parquet floor in the living room. He would take us to the army store and pay for a small pump stove for us to fix our breakfasts on, and the 10 Kg. gas cylinders to run it, and any other essentials that could be found there (with our money, of course).

Reg and Semi had a nice double bed in storage that they would love to lend us. They also offered us a powerful 220-volt transformer for any appliances we got. Our tape recorder that we had brought was for 110 volts, and that's what the apartment had, so we didn't think we would have any use for it. There were a number of different things they lent us during our stay. They convinced us that we wouldn't need a TV -- we wouldn't know what they were saying anyway -- so if we came over for the 8PM news to watch it with them, we'd have "built-in translation!"

Friends we had met at church, also helped to furnish our apartment with a couple of chests of drawers, a small wardrobe and rugs for the other rooms. We would still have to buy a living room set. of sofa and two chairs, We found a wood framed sofa with foam rubber seat and back. The price had not been changed during the latest inflation rise and included delivery! It had a pull out bed under the sofa for guests. The maroon pattern went nicely with the borrowed rugs.

Our first floor apartment had been used by a real estate business. There was one large room to the left off the building's entry hall. A large picture window, flanked by two smaller vent windows in the living room, presented a view on the front of the building, of a taxi stand and two tiny food stores across the street. The taxi stand's small office was located between the two, with the cars parked where there were spaces. This was to be our scenery.

Inside the large room, the kitchen door was on the right, opposite the windows. It stretched back like a thin dark hall. There were no appliances, but nice cabinets, newly installed, and a small window at the far end. Across from the entry door was a little hall with doors to the bathroom on the right, one bedroom straight ahead which had quite a large window that looked into the light well. On the left, the second bedroom had a picture window matching the one in the living room.

The apartment building was six stories high, but since it was built on the side of a hill, we climbed a few steps at the front, and entered apartment #7. There were two floors beneath us. Those living on the bottom floor could come out on the side street onto a sidewalk lower down the hill. It was heated with radiators, burning fuel oil. They had just changed over from coal two years before. There was a world energy crisis going on, so ten days after we moved in the fuel oil ran out. The only people really warm that winter of 1979-80 burned coal or wood. We moved in on December 21st and were not able to buy any more fuel oil until March 25th.

Our friends from church heard that we were cold. Annie, the church secretary lent us a small radiating heater with a 220V unit in it. It had been stored away for years, and she warned us we would have to put in a new coil, because it was old and rusted. We would have to change it ANYWAY for a 110V. unit -- if we could find it--since it was for 220V. Another reason for prayer! It was good language practice to go to hardware stores and explain what we wanted to buy.

Then, when the energy crisis affected the electric power supply and every day there were long cuts; our newly fixed heater was of no help. The pastor said, "There is an extra butane heater that the church is not using because there is no gas cylinder. Would you like to borrow it?" We accepted and asked when we could take it home. He said, "Come on over to the house, and I'll get it out right now."

Since the church was nine long blocks from our home, we tried to hail a taxi on the street. However, when they saw that we wanted to put the heater in the trunk, even though it didn't have a cylinder of gas, they wouldn't take us. Can you imagine us trundling this thing along on its little wheels over the cobblestones? A legalist might have said we were working on Sunday, but we felt we were carrying our "salvation" with us. Fortunately, the sergeant was happy to secure a 30 Kg. cylinder at the army store, and we bought some warm blankets at the same time.

Then, as the fuel crisis became more severe, sometimes it would take a week to get our cylinder refilled. The only place you could buy another cylinder was at the black market next to the Grand Bazaar. It was called a "Black Market," but it wasn't illegal. The police were all around the place – not to arrest either buyers or sellers -- but just to keep order in the waiting lines.

There was a little rack on the front of the stove, which would hold our newly acquired, antique copper teakettle. When we had to fire up the heater, the kettle was always there filled with water to make our breakfast cocoa, or our tea. When we returned to our thoroughly chilled apartment after language school on a snowy day, we would also strip off our wet socks and put them before the gas heater to dry. We would fill our hot water bottle and climb between flannel sheets to thaw out and study there until the apartment temperature had moderated a little. God helped us survive.

God does not cooperate on a once in a while basis. It's an all or not at all relationship. You either trust him or you don't. Running from refuge to refuge calling for Him will not bring his help if your refuge is in lies or deception. He is a God of truth. Everyone knew we were Christians. We tried always to act like it. Paul said, "Be anxious for nothing. But... let your requests be known to God." (Philippians 4:6) and it works!

Look, I stand at the door...
Rev. 3:20

9

FOOD AFOOT

You've heard of "Meals on Wheels", haven't you?

How about "Food Afoot"? We discovered that in Turkey.

Zehra hanim cooked in her own kitchen for ten families. When noontime came, Mustafa bey delivered it. Fortunately, we moved into a house just five doors from her soon after we engaged her services, so we were first in line. It came hot to our door.

We had had no facilities for preparing food, and were eating out all the time. At noon we were surviving on some light snack food for a pittance, while at night we found that we were having to dine on T-bone steak, filet mignon, duck under glass--or some such at fifty times the price.

Needless to say we were thrilled to meet Zehra hanim. We went with our Turkish landlady, Pillar, who spoke English, to visit her. Seems she sent one meat dish and two vegetable dishes every day. Dessert came only one day in four. A "portion" was enough to feed a family of five. We tried to talk her into sending us a half portion, but she said it was too much trouble.

So we had a great home cooked meal hot at noon. In the evening, most things were equally delicious cold. We often invited Pillar hanim to join us for the week we were with her until we moved into our apartment. There was always a lot left over. There was no way we could finish off that much between the two of us.

For the next fifteen months we enjoyed authentic Turkish cuisine. The subtle seasonings enhanced each meat, vegetable, and casserole. Salad was not provided usually, because she only "cooked". However, when a meal was traditionally served with a particular salad, there was often a note with it for the foreigners detailing what you needed to make it yourself.

You have probably noticed that our big problem was too much food. We started inviting friends home to help us finish it off. We often took a fellow student home from language school. Sometimes, supper as well, also provided sharing opportunities. If we couldn't take someone home to at least one meal a day, we would finish the week with several half full bowls in our wee cooler.

While still staying with Jay and Kay in those first three weeks, we joined them at Thanksgiving dinner. There were 17 present, and after a short stay in our new apartment, we found that one family we had met there were living only a couple of blocks down the hill from us. They had two wee ones, and were looking forward to a third the next summer.

When they heard that the heating had gone off in our building, and I had to wash everything in cold water by hand, they invited me to visit them on washday and use their washing machine. This we took them up on, and thought it was a marvelous time to share our left over food. They had a small wood stove in the living room for a heater, which always had a teakettle on it as well. A two burner electric hot plate served for meal preparation in the kitchen. Dee turned out some fabulous meals, and the fellowship was terrific.

Their washing machine was a little German model that also used cold water, but it wasn't freezing your hands as well. Dee had a broom stick that she used to handle the clothes with. I still had to hang up the clothes, but there was a clothesline out the window to hang them on, and then I could close the window and run back to the fire. It was much less traumatic there.

I got hold of a book about this time, *The Hiding Place*, by Corrie Ten Boom. I had heard of it for years, but hadn't ever read it before. She talked about one of the things that made her suffering in the prison camp more bearable.

She said that she offered her pain as a sacrifice to Jesus. She said it didn't really make it hurt any less, but it made her more conscious of His presence with her there. It was as though He were sharing her pain. She said it made her understand what Paul meant about the "fellowship of his suffering". Now, in memory, it seems like such a petty thing -- but when I was washing those things in that cold water, kneeling beside the bath tub, my hands hurting so badly and my tears mingling with the wash and rinse water, it was a BIG thing. It was after I made the choice to give MY pain to Jesus as a sacrifice; that He gave me a way out. He did it by giving us this family.

We later learned that it was a two-way blessing because the family had not been able to clear their support income through the bank for four months that winter. Yet, we were all well fed and warm, God providing for both of us!

We passed that terrible winter having one day a week together and enjoyed "grand-parenting" their children. We enjoyed reading to Joy and Michael and getting them ready for bed, once in a while. We heard the recitations when they were preparing for a special program in the Turkish school. We prayed with them when there was a problem. We mended things when their mother didn't have time. We ooh-ed and aah-ed over the good grades they received on their report cards.

In July we rejoiced with them when David was born. A couple of months later, Dee's mother and Mickey's mother, both came for a visit. Dee invited me over to meet the grandmothers. We had a lovely tea together, but I wondered how they felt about the show of affection when Joy climbed up and snuggled into my lap. I soon found out, because she turned that bright innocent, face up and looked into mine, and asked," Are you really my grandmother or are they?" I was a little embarrassed, but they both assured her--and me that they were very grateful that God had sent a Grandmother to love them when they were so far away. So I said, "When they go home, we can "play like" again. And we did.

When we are one body, one's particular function is not as important as the totality of the larger US. One does his job right and since we are all one, we will all be healthy and happy. Being the body of Christ provides a life full of joy and contentment.

Marshall & Hazel Thompson

The man of integrity walks securely, but he who takes crooked paths will be found out.
Proverbs 10:9

10

GETTING WHERE YOU'RE GOING

AFTER READING ABOUT "BEDLAM ON BUSES", maybe you thought buses were the only way to go. But let's begin with private cars: from the lowly Volkswagen Beetle, to the longest stretch Mercedes limousine; from funereal black to pristine white and every color on the spectrum in between; from stately antiques or barely crawling jalopies to bandbox new, just off the line; from every car maker on the globe; from spick and span clean to back country, mud-caked dirty; you'll find them all in Istanbul!

You won't find AAA in Turkey, but there is an active auto club there. We had international drivers licenses, so never bothered to get a residents license, but we did ask about a rulebook, and were told it was out of print. Every driver had his own idea about the rules of the road, and exercised them as he chose. Traffic was horrendous, and cars head to head, with dented fenders and opposing drivers in a shouting match was a frequent sight on the streets of the city. In an effort to thwart thieves, there were many owners who had invested in car alarms. The shrill sirens, or harsh squawks of these were a familiar part of the background noise.

Speaking of noise, one of the memorable ones was of the trolley cars grinding along the shiny rails that ran down the center of many of the principal avenues. Several years into our time there, most of the historic cars were replaced with trolley buses, not restricted to rails. Then, those in their turn were wiped out. And though there were commuter trains on both sides of the Bosphorus, the European side now has a "Metro" system being built.

The *Tunel* was a cable car: the oldest and shortest in the world. It took a minute and a half to make the trip, which would have been a steep ten-block walk up. Going down by foot could be easier, and there was a lot to see, so everyone should try it once. The Galata Tower is on that slope, and no trip to Istanbul is complete without climbing that almost interminable, slender, flight of stairs to emerge on the balcony. It overlooks the confluence of the waters of the Straits of the Bosphorus, the Golden Horn, and the Marmara Sea. It is breath taking but so are the stairs. So take your choice of up or down to walk and the elevator for the rest. There is an elevator for the needy.

It is easy to get lost in the old town, even trying to follow a map. Don't go alone! With the traffic patterns the way they were; when you got a taxi just outside the upper station of the "Tunel" to take you to the ferry docks (because the "tunel" was closed every night in the wee hours) you descended in a round-about pattern. You drove along the avenue: you had to go on that one way street about a half mile to Taksim Square on a level plateau. Then you turned right and plunged steeply; snaking down the switch backs to the Bosphorus. Turn right again, and drive about a mile back along the Bosphorus shore. When the shoreline veered to the left, you were forced to go straight; charging into Banker's Street, which was a narrow canyon bordered by six story buildings, for several more long blocks. When you have gone as far as the taxi can take you, you are half a block below the lower entrance to the tunel. You have been driven in a lane that loops around and emerges at a circle ending nearly where you started but on another level hundreds of feet below. You have been driven in a lane that loops around and emerges at a circle ending nearly where you started but on another level hundreds of feet below. Walking down is shorter and cheaper, but not to be done at night

Sellers sitting on the sidewalks with their wares spread out on a cloth before them congest that passage to the ferry docks or the Galata Bridge. Fashionable botiques, electronic and hardware shops line your way emerging near the docks.

Others who sell watches, song sheets, newspapers or cigarettes, walk around in long coats which have these things pinned inside. They confront the passenger and open the coat, to show what they are offering. They often get on the ferry where they have the 20 minutes it takes to cross the Bosphorus to make a few turkish liras.

Passengers waiting for the ferry, crowd the terminal vieing for a places nearest the doors. When the boat docks, the 1,200 people swarm down several gang planks onto the pier and race to their next mode of transportation on the way to their destinations. Then the gates to the street are closed. The doors from the terminal are opened for those boarding for the return trip.

We were often approached by students who took advantage of the opportunity to practice their English. This also happened when we were on the buses or comuter trains. Our colleague Tom lived just near one of the bus stops, and he often invited the young people who were bold enough to approach him to his home for a cup of tea. This triggered an invitation to their homes where they made friends with the parents. The Turks are very hospitable, and serve tiny 3 or 4 ounce glasses of VERY STRONG TEA.

At the piers where you loaded the ferries, there were someone who made coffee, and others who made tea to give you a pick me up on the way home.

There were taxis everywhere and like taxis all over the world, they have a name for making the most off the tourists that they can. They have meters: make sure it is turned on.

Marshall always talked to the drivers about their work and families. You can learn a lot about people's lives and problems that way and they like to carry on a conversation, as seems customary all over the world.

Some runs have standard fares. Once you knew the fixed rate you could pay what was due and go on. Then there were the "shared taxis". Most of these were older cars that had been cut in two and stretched to accommodate nine passengers and the driver. They charged about twice what the bus did, but you could usually get there a lot faster, and a lot more comfortably than on a bus. For one thing each passenger had a seat! There were so many of these taxis, that they practically pushed each other around the fixed route that they ran.

There were some bicycles. but many of the larger avenues, roads, and boulevards excluded bicycle traffic. There were some bicycles that were used as delivery vehicles. They had a small box out front, or in a trailer ehind in which they delivered bread, or milk, or other small items. But it's a dangerous way to live in the city traffic.

There were trucks that came from nearby market gardens to supply the many outdoor markets of the city. What a confusing, colorful, noisy, wonderful flow there was mixing, vying and streaming along the roadways of Istanbul! If I've forgotten any mode of land travel, I can't imagine WHAT it could be!

There are a myriad of ways to get where you're going in Istanbul. We tried most of them at one time or another, and sometimes liked one more because it was faster, more comfortable, more convenient, or more economical than another. Choice often depends on the time of day.

Lots of people sayq there are many roads to heaven; but Jesus said, "I am the way, the truth, and the life", and the Bible says: "Neither is there salvation in any other: for there is none other name under heaven given among men, whereby you must be saved."

These are the words of the apostle Peter in Acts; Chapter 4 verse 12, when he was hauled before the authorities: arrested for healing a crippled man at the door of the Temple in the name of Jesus Christ! If you'd like to spend eternity with God in heaven, that is the only way to "get where you're going".

Whoever trusts in his riches will fall, but the righteous will thrive like a green leaf.
Proverbs 11:28

11

MONEY MADNESS

WE PASSED TWO MILITARY PATROLS of seven men each, the two forward are eight paces before the core of three followed at almost the same distance by two rearguard. Each carried his automatic rifle or machine pistol at ready. At the main square we turned in by the seated or standing guards to enter the Osmanli bank where private security guards carried both side arms and machine pistols with thick wire stock extensions, for shoulder firing, slung over their backs.

The leftists robbed another bank yesterday taking millions. Two casualties are in hospital and not expected to survive. Every month banks are robbed. It takes lots of money to maintain the expenses of arms and propaganda. Warfare is costly and money scarce.

Once in the bank we are free to enter one of the several long lines to obtain eventual service for our needs: Foreign Exchange; Deposits or Withdrawals; Utilities Bill Payments; Mortgages or Rents. Each sign indicated a separate transaction and necessarily, time in the line. Few people in our western world find banking a traumatic experience, but in some parts of the world they still do.

Documents are the basis of identity, the proof of standing and property. They advertise your freedom to negotiate or deny you the privilege of money. The more documents, the more readily you might get your permission and obtain your aims. You need seals and tax stamps on vital papers that must be in order, to gain entrance to the inner sanctum of directors and administrators that have the final approval in their hands. The list however is long: passport, personal identity card, civil resident registration, job I.D., location with postal and telephone numbers, and -front and profile- official pictures taken in the approved photo studio. Some bureaus, offices and departments demand marriage certificates, education levels with appropriate diplomas, and even health cards.

Take a book along or even a snack to help pass the time. Remember that rudeness will not advance your cause. Always be pleasant and try to smile, the people who attend you are as tired as you of all the fuss and bother. They have this every day. It's their job and a living. Their interests and worries are likely elsewhere.

We are in the bank to get money. If you write a check on a bank outside the country they will take it and let you know when it is cleared, in ten days or a month. The post office is in chaos so you will have to drop around again, regularly. We tried to open an account with a monthly sum on call from Canada. It broke down after a few months. Osmanli Bank felt sorry for us and at one point in time gave us an account number where we could draw once a month, but the sum they assigned us was very small and the money ended before the month did.

"The money you reported as expected any day has not arrived. Perhaps it was missent?"

"Does that bank have dealings with the Chicago Central Bank? All our dealings must be channeled through them."

"Canada? Sit over there please, while I clear a line."

"We have to charge for telex. The answer could be here tomorrow. Sometimes it takes only an hour or so. Will you wait?"

"Personal checks must be initialed by one of our managers."

"Sent to you by mail? We never cash cheques 60 days after the date. Could you ask for a new issue? You'll have to return it to your home bank if they are more permissive in their policies."

"Your emergency fund was invested by agreement at 75% interest for the first three months. After that it reverted to the regular rate of 50% for the rest of the year. I'm sorry you're $75. short of the original total. You know how the currency is devaluating, you must have read the agreement thoroughly."

"Our Bank allows only one withdrawal each month in that kind of account. You'll have to wait."

"We don't cash that kind of Travelers Checks here. We can only handle this company's business. Perhaps the Cotton Bank will change it for you. You've already tried them?"

"I'm sure I don't know."

"We can't do that."

"Sorry."

We were sitting in the Osmanli Bank one day and heard "Marshall Thompson" being paged. When we went to investigate we were informed that a money order was waiting in a bank across Taksim Square, which they could not handle because they had no agreement with the source bank in Canada. When we collected it we were informed that it had been there for two months.

We met many cordial bank managers. Some of them were men of God, others worldly but pleasant; men who know their trade. We drank a small glass of tea or a demitasse of Turkish coffee, the essential lubricant of all commercial dealings and talked of our lives. One Turk had studied in Paris. His mother was American so he went to the Fleur de Lys Protestant church where the people's faces shone. Another foreigner was an elder in his Scottish home church. Those who had studied abroad had English and a good impression of Christianity. Their social position precluded any outward expression of faith in the secular climate prevalent in Turkey. However, I caught one reading a small New Testament in his office so I prayed for him there at that moment. Because he initialed my checks, I owed my friend my best.

For faith to be effective it needs to be bold. We were frequently very low on money but we never missed a meal. As Jesus promised His provision is always complete each moment. You can bank on it!

*Prepare your shields, both large and small,
and march out for battle!*
Jeremiah 46:3

12

THREE MINUTES SILENCE

TIME 9:05, NOVEMBER 10, L980: Sirens sounded, traffic slowed, stopped and people got out of their cars. Pedestrians looked at each other and quieted. Our guests gave us questioning looks. We had been hurrying to catch a bus, and there were many lined up a few meters away on the busiest street in Istanbul, but they were clearly not doing any immediate business. It was evident that the heart of the city had stopped.

John and Virginia were visiting us almost a year after our arrival to announce the approval of our project. We too had stopped and were facing a band that had been playing vigorously. Though we had not seen it, we knew what was going on. Ataturk, father of Modern Turkey, had breathed his last at 9:05 on November 10, 1938. Now 42 years later, Istanbul, a city of eight or ten million people, even a whole nation of fifty five million--was paralyzed commemorating that moment with three minutes of silence.

Just across the six lane Cumhurriet Boulevard from where we were caught, was the Ordu Evi -- the officers club -- where the elite honor guard lived, operated, and were housed. All the important guests of the state were accommodated here while visiting in Turkey's #1 city. Visible to us, and all who were frozen in time at that juncture, was the honor guard in their precise formation, standing at attention. When the three minutes had passed, they moved with the stiffness required to carry out the ceremony of lowering the flag to half-mast, where it would hang for the rest of the day.

We watched spellbound, and wished for a camera, to record this historic moment. We whispered, "If there is a God in Turkey today, his name is Ataturk."

The principal of a Muslim private high school asked a key question. "In the schools of America do they have a picture of Washington in every class room?" Marshall's answer was, "Perhaps one in the entrance hall or the principal's office. Usually one or two to a school." He shook his head in exasperation. "Here we have to show at least one picture of Ataturk in every room." The authorities don't like private religious schools and try to shut them down if they neglect any by-law.

His image is everywhere: schoolrooms, business offices, train stations. His sayings are quoted on the media, offered for sale as posters, plaques and banners in every print shop, and occasionally spelled out on some hillside with whitewashed stones burnt grass. Each week all the public schools have an assembly day. The programs prepared for those days are full of small children quoting the catchy axioms of Ataturk which fit that particular time of year, like: "He can count himself lucky who calls himself a TURK." The Newspaper printed commemorative poems written about him on that special day of his death. But the flowery tributes offered by the children that day had been memorized with care weeks ahead of time and were ALL dedicated to him.

Some years later, I experienced another exaggerated demonstration of this adulation. I sat in the doctor's office awaiting my appointment. It was the Marmara University Hospital. Two lovely Turkish ladies came in and chose to sit on either side of me and chat. They both spoke English, were dressed in the latest Paris fashions, with professionally arranged hair. They were each married to a distinguished doctor, who headed his department. We discussed the beauty of the Istanbul parks, the hospitality of the citizens, and problems of the current government.

Then suddenly, the outside door opened, and in came a lady in a "*chador*" (that black robe worn all over the Middle East) covering her from head to toe. My new friends leaned forward, to look at each other, and almost in unison said, "I never thought I'd see the day that a daughter of Ataturk would dress like that!"

In our first year and a half in Turkey we had seen only four ladies so dressed. However, days before our arrival, Iran had instituted an Islamic Revolution taking 53 U.S. hostages, and holding them for 440 days before finally releasing them. In the intervening years Turkey had been inundated with propaganda by the Ayatola Khomeni. He called on "decent women" to "cover themselves and separate themselves from the godless secular government and return to the true faith." One of the reforms of Ataturk had been to ban those very "*chadors*" for women, and the red *fez* for men. He even tried to outlaw the "*shalvar*"! (the baggy pants).

The only time you saw the "shalvar" in Istanbul was when the cleaning lady was leaning out, washing the 5th story window. No one could accuse HER of being indecent! Also, perhaps Grandma was visiting from the village and would have on her "Sunday best" velvet. Probably, back in the village she wore this very comfortable attire all the time! After all, who would arrest Grandma? But of course, the grandchildren learn about Ataturk in school.

Everybody my age and younger, had learned to read Turkish written in Latin script--and Turkey has the highest literacy rate among the Islamic nations. Before Ataturk changed the alphabet in 1928, the language had been written in Arabic script. Literacy had been near ten percent.

Every year in every grade a paper is written by every scholar on the life, exploits, thoughts or inspiration provided by the national hero. Teachers evaluated each composition and consulted with each student. They graded carefully for commendations and awards. All this was done for a man who saved their nation from destruction and dissolution.

We are told of a day coming at the judgment seat of Christ where our works and words of devotion will be judged. Where commendations and awards will be given. This, for and by the God-Man who has saved His people from destruction and dissolution brought on by sin and despair. Surely He is worthy of infinitely greater devotion and love.

Marshall & Hazel Thompson

*Go and proclaim... I remember the devotion
of your youth; how as a bride you loved me.*
Jeremiah 2:2

13

SURVIVAL TESTING

THE MINIBUS GROUND TO A halt at a roadblock established by a group of Turkish soldiers. Two men with submachine guns at ready mounted the bus. The young officer commanded that we produce our passports. I translated this into stilted bookish French. My wife and I had studied Turkish for six months, while the French tourists we traveled with had only been here a few days. This trip had been our family joke - Did we have survival level Turkish? We had not meant it to be taken literally. But these men were looking for subversives or propagandists. The revolutionary Islamic government in neighboring Iran had imprisoned American hostages. Revolutions can spread if inflamed by clever arguments and appeals to deep historic prejudices. Books written in the Arabic alphabet or Cyrillic were forbidden. A book in Kurdish could get you shot!

Audiotapes could not be sent across the border or received from abroad. For decades all Kurdish language classes had been forbidden in all schools despite the large concentrations (approximately five million,) of these people in the east. All Kurdish radio stations were over the border in other neighboring countries. Resentments had prepared the ground that awaited a spark to catch. Government troops were everywhere. Everything and everyone was suspect.

Insurrection was at hand and the fighting between socialist leftists and the conservative rightists continued. Efforts were made to hide the effects to the outsiders but the conflict consisted of continuous local clashes between small groups of hit and run activists; painting slogans on walls; robbing banks for arms purchases; avenging public denunciations by the opposing parties' outstanding men. Some killed for politics, others for more personal reasons, under the guise of politics.

Our survival test started with a boat trip to Samsun and Trabzon on the Black Sea and then a coastal bus ride to Artvin. We visited Ani an ancient ruin on the Soviet border and were warned by the guide not to take pictures lest the guards in the towers across the frontier be seen. Later we hitchhiked on a truck back to Erzurum in the high mountains. We were required to talk constantly for all kind of reasons and also to explain the pictures we took along of our two daughters' weddings. They proved better than a letter of introduction as we repeatedly used them on drivers and travelers.

We found no commercial links to Van city with it's carbonated water of the nearby lake. Then we met the French tour and the Turkish driver permitted us, for cash, to ride along with them.

Our French friends looked bored as they produced their documents. Our passports were different, we were not part of the tour, would that make for difficulties? We had been within a stone's throw of the Iranian border twice. Where we were invited by the tour master to put our foot over the line to say we had trod another country's soil. But each time we had declined, by saying "Fifty-three hostages is enough!" The tourists laughed at the reply of the quaint professor and his cute, petit wife.

The officer examined each passport with care and looked several times between the picture and the person with each document. He lingered before a handsome dark eyed young woman in the seat across the aisle and addressed some words to her. I realized that she would not understand so I explained that they all spoke French only. His eyes widened in surprise. He shook his head, what a pity. He eyed our passports hurriedly, and with a last, soulful backward glance from the door, departed. The woman, who knew she had somehow pleased, smiled shyly to herself. Perhaps she was wondering at the thrill attraction gives to routine. The universal romantic search for the imagined ideal companion had changed the order of events.

I later concluded that the lady was the granddaughter of some Armenian refugee to France. But for the Turkish persecution of her people during the First World War there might have been a romantic ending to traditional barriers of hatred between races and religions.

I breathed a sigh of relief as our scrutinizers signaled our freedom to proceed on our trip. Our friends would not be detained unduly by the presence of two strangers from North America. God had proven again that He could see us through our adventure. God saves not only our soul but frequently our skin and in this case our time and that of our hosts. The romantic attraction that disrupted the official routine is akin to that which animates our search for cause and meaning in life. We may be distracted for a moment, but we want the real thing. If God is, we want to know Him, but we are nervous about it. Suppose He wants us to do something we don't want to do? We have to be reassured. He loves us, but wants changes. We are timid, although anything He wants will be a pleasure. Our delight will be in His commands. It's hard to believe until you experience it.

Trust in the Lord and do good…
Psalm 37:3

Marshall & Hazel Thompson

*You live in the midst of deception;
in their deceit they refuse
to acknowledge me.*
Jeremiah 9:6

14

BORDER INCIDENT

To stay in a country you need a visa in your passport authorizing you to a certain number of days in their country. Tourist visas are common, but a resident visa was another matter, a very difficult and often refused procedure. After three months on a tourist visa renewal was required and the easiest way to get one was to cross the border and reenter the country. The Greek border was the closest and the most used by European and other tourists. That is where they expected you to enter.

Our very FIRST experience across this border had been with a friend who offered to take us in his car. It was a sort of "show us the ropes" trip. There were many shortages at the time: coffee, cocoa, evaporated milk, light bulbs, toilet tissue, mustard, oatmeal; to name a few. There were always some people who wanted us to bring back some strong drink. Though we steadily refused on that score, those people just kept on asking us every single time we went!

On that trip the banks were not open, and we were only able to get a very limited amount of cash in "drachmas" at the post office, so had no trouble explaining why we couldn't bring back much. Our friend introduced us to a storeowner who could speak Turkish (so we wouldn't have to deal in Greek) and accepted Turkish currency or US dollars. We were expecting to change a fairly large travelers check, and had brought only about US$10, and very little in Turkish Lira. Many things had familiar brand labels, and I think that we were never surprised at the contents when we opened a can.

After we were in Greece, had finished our shopping, and our driver had finished his visiting; he explained that he was going to smuggle some booklets across, with us sitting on the seat where they were hidden. It proved educational. Although we are usually very chicken about breaking the law we went along with the idea. We had read how Brother Andrew had moved Scriptures for the Lord across Communists' borders. Wouldn't this be the same? We saw that we lacked faith, but rallied.

Actually, The final disposition of the purchased goods filled the back of the station wagon where the seat was folded down. However, the middle seat was left upright so I could sit there. Marshall sat with our friend up front. The booklets were on the floor behind the driver, well covered with the toilet tissue club pack: a carton of 48, and the small tote bag in which we had our purchases of the day.

We returned to the border with some trepidation. At the border, most people got out to stretch their legs, use the facilities, maybe get a candy bar and a bottle of pop, but we took our purchased goods and passports into the customs building. Our friend who spoke Turkish fluently joined us with his car permit. The customs people decided to look over the car and we accompanied them. They set the things out of the car, and when they got to the booklets, took them inside, saying we could put everything back now. I stayed there and started to repack the car.

Our friend went inside to protest, protect and recover the booklets, if possible. Marshall followed to see what would happen. I could imagine him arrested, the car impounded, and us having to return on the bus. I did a lot of praying in those moments.

The customs officers took the booklets out, sorted through them, left them scattered on the table. There were many truck drivers waiting for six o'clock. They were not allowed to drive their big 18 wheelers on that road into Istanbul until evening. Here was a real diversion! Some were really curious--they each snatched up one or two--and began leafing through them. They had heard "religious propaganda" mentioned, so they flipped right to the back of the book and one said, "There it is right there. They want you to receive Jesus." "Yeah, they say you can't get to Paradise without Jesus." Most stuffed their pockets with several of each different kind before they went away.

Meanwhile our friend was trying to show the officials that this was not political, and was not going to hurt anybody. The officers were making out a receipt that they said he could take into the customs offices in downtown Istanbul, and if there was nothing wrong with it, they would give him back his box of booklets.

Our friend never got his literature back. But, you know what I imagine, now? I visualize him in heaven, some day. A Turkish man he doesn't recognize rushes up to him, greets him like family, and thanks him. Our friend asks, "Whatever for?" "Well, it was back in the 80's. I was driving through from Germany. When the agents searched your car, I and all my buddies wondered what it was about and trooped in to see what was going on. We figured you'd probably never get it back anyway, and just helped ourselves to those little booklets.

"I took mine home and read every word. I had some questions, and went down the street from where I live in Germany to a little church. They were happy to answer my questions. I got into a Bible study, and took my wife along and finally we came to Jesus. Thanks again"

Teach me your ways, O Lord...
Psalm 27:11

Watch your life and doctrine closely,
Persevere in them, because if you do, you will
save both yourself and your hearers.
1st Timothy 4:16

15

THE MUSLIM BOYS' SCHOOL

It was evident from the start that according to Turks the only thing we Westerners had to offer them was wealth and technology. They felt they were religiously and culturally superior, but to get our technology and wealth required language skills. This they were willing to get from us. But they considered us dangerous teachers to be cared for, appreciated, but to be watched as potential troublemakers. History indicated that the rebellion and freedom of the Balkan nations was traceable to the preparation of future leaders of those nations at Roberts College and other training agencies of Protestant and Catholic education. Not that this was a conscious aim of the institutions, but an unforeseen byproduct.

Such institutions are largely supervised or controlled by government now. In this way they can prohibit chapel or Bible study programs. Superior education within the limits of home culture and religion seemed a reasonable goal. Ataturk, the father of the nation, had favored secularism, which minimized religion. This was now state policy. They helped build mosques and pay *imam*s a salary to give them some control. Naturally, many Turks who were religious disagreed with the government position. Some tried to start or promote top educational institutions that would uphold and support Islam. But they would need to teach one of the required foreign languages: English, French or German, besides the language of the Koran, Arabic.

I had already prayed Turkhan through three jobs. I also paid him to give me Turkish lessons between jobs. Turkhan had been converted at 18 by my friend Howard. When he took a trip, I would be instructed to "look after Turkhan while I'm away." It was something easier said than done. But at this moment he had reached a point of equilibrium and his family was reconciled, his marriage went well and the baby was growing. This third job was as a secretary in a Muslim High School with a dormitory for those from out of town. They wished to outdo Roberts College and other secular institutions of fame as a zealous but modern education "lycee".

As Turkhan explained it, they had problems not only with the state education department, but also with the project of teaching more courses in English. They hadn't enough knowledgeable teachers in that subject. To reach their goal they decided to get an English teacher to teach their teachers. The prime worry of the Principal was that they would have to put up with a foreigner who smoked and drank. A definite downer for a school promoting Islam and having dozens of students who would see his depraved life style and perhaps be influenced. Turkhan had mentioned my name as an experienced candidate who fit their need. I was a bit disturbed by this news. Would God want me to help an Islamic school? Was it an opportunity or a bad choice? I decided I was willing and left it in His hands. The next day it was dramatically decided.

I was advised by phone that my interview was at 3PM and a chauffeur and car would pick me up at 2:30. It was a limousine and the uniformed driver got me across town in record time. The office was impressive; the director was impressive; and the building was impressive. They offered me the same salary as a full time Turkish teacher without any of the extra duties of dorm, study hall or recess supervision. I would teach all those professors committed to learn English for three mornings each week from nine to twelve. An advanced and beginners level was already prepared. That was impressive. They offered me free breakfast and lunch. I was overwhelmed and had no arguments against the project. God evidently approved.

The problem was the daily trip across town. If I caught the tram, five blocks from our house, before 7:30 I could be sure of a seat and I got to the school in time for breakfast with the staff. If I missed it, I would be lucky to get there on time for class. My tram took me across the Golden Horn and up past the aqueduct to a bypass under a main thoroughfare. I got off and caught another bus or a tram in order to descend at the door of the school. The eight o'clock tram was an hour later because of the increase in traffic. The 8:30 tram put me an hour late to the first class. I was late for class only once but I missed breakfast a number of times.

The first breakfast I decided I had to bow my head and pray before eating. It was my custom. Pray and be labeled religious? Well, I was and why hide a good thing? They picked up on it immediately. "You believe in God!" a teacher said in English. "I obey the Messiah Isa (Jesus)." I replied in Turkish. They nodded their heads in approval. They had struck a gold mine, a religious westerner. But one young man wanted to set me straight, so at a break later in the week, he came to talk.

"There is ONE God" he maintained. He must have argued with Christians of Orthodox faith, because you could tell he was waiting to hear the negative. "No, there is a Trinity." Then we could have gone back and forth: "three; one; three; one; THREE! ONE!" And each gone home saying: Thank God, I know He is one or Thank God, I know He is a Trinity. Both would be right and no light would have been shed in either mind. So I shocked him. "Yes, one great wonderful United God." They use the word *birlik*, made one, as for bus companies or united enterprises where several corporations or owners get together and pool their stock, buses or personnel. I was intimating that God was not a solitary but a compound One. The novelty of the concept killed his prepared arguments. To his amazement the Christian had admitted to one God. He didn't know where to go from there and I went back to class feeling good.

In the rec room, where you could buy sandwiches, cookies, tea or pop, etc., was a table for table tennis. Evidently normal school graduates are as accomplished as seminary students at the game. My first game, however, showed me what I was up against. My adult Engllish students were their teachers. They were all good ping pong players; no pushovers here!1q The students, about ten years old, gathered to watch rather like a contest with a rival school. They groaned when I made a point and chattered excitedly when a teacher pulled ahead. It was a joust, a tourney; the winner upheld the rightness of Islam and a loss to the infidel was a tragedy. How do you reduce such a game to fun and relaxation?

I was a better player than they had counted on, but there were some sharp men among my best teachers. I played vigorously and shouted my enjoyment when I aced something, or missed the ace. I complimented them on keen shots. I celebrated loudly when I won or when they won. I made it obvious that I placed little value on winning, but much on a game well played. It became fun. They stopped worrying. Within a week the attitude and atmosphere in the rec room at game time had changed. They watched, talked or simply ignored us as they played with their friends. It was only a game.

Although I used English with my students I also got the benefit of new Turkish words. One student wanted to know the English for *ayva* when I looked it up it was 'quince'. Then I got the phrase: 'You make us eat quince.'; a Turkish way of saying, "You give us bitter medicine." or "this subject is tough".

After the first week they were at ease enough to ask questions. Good sharp questions about Western society at first, then religious views. The classes were an opportunity and a challenge. My students were amazed to learn that the problems they face in a secular world are the same as religious Christians face in the Western world where religious values are alternately attacked, praised or generally ignored. The students were not the only questioners. One day the principal asked me how many pictures of George Washington would be displayed in American Schools. I replied that in the U. S. possibly one in an entrance or large hall. In Canada one or two of the Queen. He reminded me of the obvious, every room has to carry one of several acceptable pictures of Ataturk. I told him the practice was more like religious pictures in a Catholic or Orthodox school. He asked if there was a big difference between boys who attended church and those who didn't. I replied that, "Yes, boys who attend church fear God and respect elders." He remarked that it was the same in Istanbul. Mosque boys were easier to teach and more dutiful and attentive. "For the same reasons," I laughed: "The fear of God bears the same fruit. Respect for all."

I got to tell my teachers that Baptists believed in a spiritual rebirth. That we baptized people after they were old enough to reason. Once when we were meeting during an electric cut, I announced that we were due to have an exercise on audiotape next, so I had prayed for power to be restored. The lights came on that moment. I didn't ask what they thought of that. When I spoke of the early persecutions of Baptists in Europe they sympathized. "You poor people are almost like us Muslims. We know how terrible those Christians are".

I found out how to get Scripture to them. Never give anything to your students, but after they are out of your class and into someone else's you could show appreciation by a special gift. A Scripture calendar to one; an English New Testament to another, but never a multiplicity for "propaganda": each must be tailored for a friend. Never give a New

Testament in Turkish, it would be considered proselytizing, they have to get that for themselves.

There was a very intelligent and sensitive *imam* or religious teacher at the school, popular with the boys. He knew no English and was not my student, but we had talked at free time. At the end of the year, I took a pocket New Testament with Psalms in Arabic, the language he taught, and slipped it into his pocket at lunch. I told him that I appreciated him and his work and would like to give him something to read at home. He thanked me, but did not look at it there. He will treasure it for the language, if not for the foreign friend.

Several of the very best of my teachers were competent enough to take on the task of teacher for some of the beginners. The second term in January I had fewer students and they were slightly less able than my advanced class had been before.

There was a flurry of gossip when my secretary friend, Turkhan, was found to have Christian books about the Old Testament prophets in his locker at school. Some said he was making propaganda. He became hysterical and needed psychiatric intervention. We had had days off for spring break. When I saw him I told him he was silly to get upset. They were my books bought and brought from North America. He had but to tell them whose they were and that he was keeping them for me. They expected me to be Christian. I had intended the books for the library, I had supposed Muslims would be interested in other prophets, but it turned out that only one interested them: Mohammed, who titled himself the last and greatest. They sum up Jesus and the others by saying their messages were all the same: repent and worship Allah. Mohammed stated that God is angry with the Jews and will never smile on them again. This is why the nation of Israel is such an affront to religious Muslims. The Jews rule and prosper. If the nation of Israel continues to prosper Islam's prophet is wrong and his believers are too. Saint Paul stated that Jews will, in the last days, be reconciled to Christ. This has not yet been realized. On such things hang the faith of multitudes.

...knock and the door will be opened...
Mathew 7:7

16

VERIFYING VISAS

"WHEN YOU GO TO THIS city in Northern Greece to renew your visa, you go to the Turkish consulate for an English teaching visa at the Institute." We couldn't believe our supervisor's words. We had tried to get recognition and permission to teach from the Turkish embassy on a visit to Egypt months before. Could a consulate have more power than an embassy in direct contact with Ankara? But we were desperately tired of departing for a stay in Greece or Cyprus every three months. Something fun in spring or summer could be quite a drag in the autumn rains or winter snows on bus or van.

During our first term in Istanbul, we did not even try to get a residence visa. A tourist visa lasted three months, and then you could get a bus to the Greek border, cross and have a cup of coffee, shop, walk back across, and they stamped a new three month visa into your passport; just like that! Our first trip we went with a friend, in his car. Across the border he pointed out hotels where we could stay, and gave us a general orientation. Subsequent trips we took on buses that went to the border. We walked across, and caught a local bus into the nearest town of Alexandropolis. Then we found a hotel, went and did some shopping. It was always something of an adventure, a time for rest, and buying some things that you couldn't get in Turkey.

A young American family we knew liked oatmeal. They asked that we be on the lookout for Quaker Oats. Well, we recognized that Quaker on the can, and each time managed to bring them at least one. I'm not sure what country it was packed in, but it was really packed in tight. Later we found that it was sometimes available in Istanbul, and we bought them a few packages at a time when we found it in the supermarket. However, even though the package was much larger, it was loosely packed, had some impurities in it, and was only available just after harvest. Once I went to another branch of the popular MIGROS SUPERMARKET, and thought I'd see if they had any oatmeal. The girl showed me the stuff, and then asked me in a whisper, what do you do with it? I assured her that you cooked it like cream of wheat, which Turks eat, too: but sweetened and with milk, for breakfast.

Cyprus was an alternative visa exit, providing a mix of exciting dimensions for it was a vacation land "par excellence". You could drive through the countryside and see lots of significant ruins, lead an active life with swimming, boating and sports or visits to sea and mountain parks. You could also just spend your time shopping or resting in ideal circumstances. The British had left a great material blessing from the colonial period in the improved state of roads, buildings, ruins and museums. The Anglican Church was warmly functional and the Catholic open for the expatriates and tourists with government permission. However, politics required that the Greek Orthodox Church be treated as a museum and not for meetings.

Sleep came without care and strain or the noise of machine gun fire. The United Nations kept the peace between the two sides of the divided island. However, we never tried to visit the other side of the island. After all, the little Turkish Republic created by the army had taken 36% of the island and over 50% of the best agricultural land for the Turkish 20% of the original population. Immigration from the mainland had now made native-born Turks a minority in their part of the island. Even the capitol was divided and a great tourist attraction was the viewing of the line of division from the roof garden of a tall central hotel building. If one visited the Greek part of the island you were not allowed to return to the Turkish side. Retaliation for visits to the north side could come at the Turkish-Greek border the next time you took that means of going out for your visa--as one of our young friends found out when she was strip-searched by female Greek border police. Her crime? She had let the Cyprus airport police stamp her passport, admitting her to Turkish-controlled North Cyprus. We asked them to stamp a paper tucked into the passport document. They always complied; it could be removed before passing to Greece on some later trip. The ways of diplomacy are devious and many an innocent falls thereby.

We learned so many things the hard way, by unpleasant experiences. An expensive visa and lots of red tape kept people out of Communist Bulgaria. One trip I decided I'd like to see across the border by returning to Turkey via the city of Edirne, the historic, ancient city of Adrianopolis where many battles were fought in ancient and modern times. One road led north of our usual entry point. A narrow appendix of land separated Greece, Bulgaria and Turkey. Each clung to the river that divided them.

We had exited late from Turkey to Alexandropolis but decided to leave the next day without shopping. We left early on a little minibus carrying Greek farmers home. It took several hours to get to the Border crossing. We got off at the exit and left the Greek side walking and carrying our suitcases across the bridge. The border marker was at the central span but the surprise awaited us in the shade at the end of the bridge. A crouching soldier stood with gun and bayonet pointed at us. We stopped and I put down the heavy bags. Another man came and called us into the office. Here the army controlled the crossing. There were not the usual inspectors and officials that occupied the main crossing down river. A man of captain's rank came and looked over our passports. He did not like what he saw.

For over a year we had been entering, staying for three months, and then crossing the border just long enough to get a new tourist visa. The bulk of traffic came through the southern checkpoint, where they usually just stamped the passport without any question. They were always so busy that they didn't have time for that. However, there were very few tourists that came through Edirne. This man decided that we had something to hide, and that was the reason that we didn't go back the way we came.

And he was determined that we weren't going to put anything over on him! First he searched our suitcases--and not finding any contraband began to shout at us. "What are you doing in Turkey? Why don't you get a residence visa? They're onto you aren't they? You knew they wouldn't give you another visa, didn't you? So you thought you'd escape by coming this way! Don't you dare come through here again!" Of course, this translation may not be very exact -- as our Turkish was not the best. Fortunately, our knowledge of the local profanity was limited. Besides, Marshall sent Hazel out of the room when the tirade began to heat up. She exited and prayed while he kept his cool and tried to convince the man our interest as tourists and teachers was historic and linguistic. Our aim was pure. We promised to get a residence permit. The lesson stuck;

we determined that when we returned from furlough our concentration would be on getting a job that had a visa. At the bus stop outside the base the late traffic was all toward Istanbul so we never got a historic tour of Edirne. We got to town very late.

Marshall applied for a job teaching English at the school where Hazel already taught. But would it get us a visa? There existed a way, arranged somehow by our language school that was not in any official guidebook or information bulletin. But it worked. When we were in Greece at the start of our second term we visited the consulate. We sent in our degrees and certificates with a form done in triplicate and waited for the interview. We chatted with the secretary who was very cordial, and enjoyed showing off his knowledge of English.

The consul sent out the signed residence visa and teaching certificate. He gave permission without even seeing us. It was as easy as that.

Life can be very easy and simple for those who follow given instructions by a knowing and caring individual. Such a one is Jesus. In this life, many are fooled by the advice they are given for living a "successful life". Their goal is enjoyment without measure, excitement, pleasure, ambition, money, sex, to be in the know, and to control others. Taste and try it all - so many impressive people say. Yet these things leave their mark and mar so many lives and minds. Some pay dearly in the present and more in the future. The value of a clean conscience and a good reputation are frequently learned the hard way. There is a verifiable salvation and visa to God's country. You have to apply for it and fulfill its conditions. It is easily possible, yet a loving, available Savior is known by so few.

Look, the fear of the Lord, that is wisdom.
Job 28:28

Whatever you do, work at it with all your heart, as working for the Lord, not for men.
Colossians 3:23

17

HOLD THAT HOLIDAY

"THE POLICE ARE INVESTIGATING US, Mrs. Thompson. They say your husband talked about religion in class. We know he would never have done that, but would you please tell him to stop. They could close our school." It was the fall of our second term. I, Marshall, was asked to substitute for one of the young Turkish teachers who had graduated from Bosphorus University, the child of Robert's College, originally an American missionary enterprise. Denuded now of its zeal for faith, it still promoted inquiring minds and openness of discussion. The young lady in question had evidently applied her concepts to politics and to her class.

The day I substituted, the lesson touched on the words: celebrate, reunion, shopping, presents, and the other activities associated with Christmas. The reading was not the Christmas story nor contained any mention of faith, but of the family celebration, the feasting and the choice, purchase, production and exchange of gifts. The problems of gathering the extended family in uncertain winter weather and the holiday rush took paragraphs of examples.

Most of the Eastern Christians in Istanbul celebrate Epiphany on Jan. 6th and exchange gifts, but we give our gifts on the 25th of December. We used to take two weeks to celebrate as witnessed to in our carol: *The Twelve Days of Christmas*. The Turks under Ataturk started celebrating New Year, halfway between the two. Legal Turkish holidays were a day off for everybody, but Christian holidays were only for, those of that faith, largely foreigners and teachers who would get these days off as well. Needless to say, the students loved, to have Christian teachers because they too would get the day off. Christmas and Good Friday were extras for the fortunate.

I wrote the date December 25th on the blackboard and we read the exercise. One of the boys on the back row was not cooperative. Something had clearly put him off. I finished the class and thought no more about it. I liked volunteering to do a class when needed for the smooth functioning of the school. But I couldn't help noticing our supervisor looked harassed and avoided talking to me the next few days. When I understood the problem I took the book, opened to the lesson and went to her office. I said I understood that there were complaints about my class and showed her the Christmas lesson. She was appalled. One of the students had denounced the school and both teachers. One talked politics and the other religion, he told police. They forced our supervisor to grant six scholarships for the policemen to attend classes to satisfy themselves that this was not true. They threatened to close the school otherwise.

We had plainclothes men and women in our midst from that time on. Should we count them as spies or special students? I opted for students since I felt that with the increase of tourists they would need all the English they could learn. My supervisor told me which of our students were police at the start of the new term. I had wondered about a man in my class before I knew he was 'my cop'. He was a serious family man, bearded, near 40 but watched me suspiciously. He acted like learning English would be only secondary so I decided to make him work hard or quit. The very first day he recognized the fact that he had to respond with the reading or words rapidly, for if he missed, the other younger students snickered. That made him pull up his socks and work. Since I ran all my classes like that, they learned or dropped out in three weeks. We would start with a full room, every seat taken and in three weeks of intensive drill and twenty or more new words a lesson, we would have four or five vacancies. The challenge to those who remained in class stimulated them to make progress. For reading we had classics and other books reduced to 800-to 1000 word basic vocabulary that they could soon read. We had ten weeks of three, two-hour classes a week, six hours totaling 60 to launch them. The full course had six books to use, it was an ideal two-year program if they kept at it. The reward was not a certificate (which the government prohibited,) but the use of a language.

The entrance tool to a world of ideas, concepts and opportunities, new and exciting for them to explore. I wanted my cop to get there.

Later learned that my cop was the chief of the political section of the police and his job was to watch for suspicious, illegal action by banned parties. I met him with his family once in summer on one of the nearby Princes' Islands where I was scuba diving. I wondered if he would think I was penetrating the nearby naval base, but we had a pleasant conversation, he considered me his teacher and introduced me with due respect to his two girls, whom he had once brought to class, and his wife. He knew my wife at the school. He took several courses under me and later met one of my Christian Turkish friends who gave me Turkish drill and Bible reading practice. They met at the British library. After they talked awhile one mentioned me as his teacher the other as his friend. They evidently spent a lot of time together and my Christian friend offered my cop a Turkish New Testament, which he took.

I had three of the plainclothes men and one policewoman in a late night class in the third year, after curfew was lifted. It was memorable because it was a fast paced, smart class and we worked hard. My police became worried when we had a lesson on Valentine's Day; the kids liked it too much. This was probably a reaction from the days when the police had a religious function. The night class was successful so we offered the course again next term. This time my cop came and was involved in one of the noisiest arguments I ever had between students. My cop thought he had been slighted when another answered his question. It was possibly my fault. In drill or dialogue if a student delayed a response I would refer it to the next student. It was a technique to keep an edge of alertness and concentration we wanted on the part of the students. A delay meant being skipped by the teacher; a downer for a "face saving" people. He had missed some classes and may have come unprepared but I showed him no special privilege although he sat on my right in the circle of chairs. Since he was in plain clothes few could know his identity. A lovely young Armenian, who sat on my left, took up the stumble when I indicated she was to go on. He objected, but the drill was six people past him. Later, when his turn came in another exercise he was to address some question to the girl; she would respond with an answer; and await a reply. Then she would address the same question to the next person on her left (a young man who escorted her to class) and repeat the same dialogue. My cop blundered on his question and did not reply, so I motioned for the question to go on and it did. He should have been angry with me, but, teachers are above criticism in Turkey. He blustered, claiming she had lost him the opportunity to respond. Angry words were exchanged from right to left, across my bow so to speak and I momentarily lost control of the class. The tea break was due at any time so I sent everyone out. The older man took her to task and the boy friend took her part. They shouted for five minutes in the corridor while I put my head on the desk and prayed. When they returned I put my hand on my cop's arm and smiled at him. I put my hand on my chest in the gesture they use when they beg pardon. Later he quietly asked to be excused and left early. I never saw my cop again.

Several years later an American colleague asked permission to have a Christmas party after the last evening class at the end of term. His class had requested it. The supervisor enthusiastically granted permission and offered refreshments. We invited all the students. Attendance was optional. It was not a regular class, the students who came wanted to sample a Western Christmas party. We felt free to have a reading of the Christmas story from Luke in the new International Version, and then a fill in the blank resumé of the story (we listed the words possible for the blank places) and let them write it in as a game.

We had handmade posters with the words to sing Jingle Bells and other carols. Everyone brought an inexpensive gift, which we exchanged by draw and opened publicly. There was much laughter and most of the students who came thought it was wonderful. I don't even remember if any of the police attended. There were no repercussions. It became a custom that continued.

Holidays define a state, culture or religion. Civil Authorities promote and set significant dates apart for public observance. Our police worried about the student's reaction to many western customs and holidays. Yet they too found charm in so many things connected to the new foreign ways. There is delight in so many of our holy days.

I have always respected police and have never been afraid of them. However, I knew little about them before my experiences in Turkey. I had little occasion before to meet or teach them. You really can learn to spot them when you know there is at least one in your class. It became a kind of game.

I have always felt it was God's purpose to make this contact because the tourist trade continued to expand as did the need for foreign languages. That the police were benefited I have no doubt. But at the moment it seemed a threat, many Christian workers taught for their residence visa. Some feared they would not be able to continue to bear witness in the country. In the English language schools and in University I met men and women teachers of sterling quality who lived a witness to their faith. We should ask ourselves how we show forth Christ-like qualities and faith in our own chosen profession -- no matter what that is or where we live.

To depart from evil, that is understanding.
Job 28:28

Marshall & Hazel Thompson

*Pray also for me, that whenever
I open my mouth, words may be given me
so that I will fearlessly make known the
mystery of the gospel…*
Ephesians 6:19

18

LET'S NOT PRETEND!

CODE IS AN IMPORTANT TOOL. We hide facts by disguising words and get the message to those for whom it was designed, leaving all others in ignorance. It's a great ego booster to know secrets that others don't know. It goes along with games like cops and robbers as a fun thing.

In the interest of brevity and truth we use abbreviations to shorten long titles. Organizations, societies, factories and governments use these shortened names to identify different agencies or items in its scope and control. It's even better if you can make them spell something associated with its function. We code many organizational activities for brevity and convenience. It also gives an intimate sense of belonging, identity and even secrecy. Abbreviations identify the participants as well as the groups, the projects or the goals. In wars a code word cloaks the actions planned against the enemy: Barbarossa, Plowshare, etc. were code words of campaigns planned by generals. Constantly changing passwords at each military base and camp identify outsiders and distinguish those from the approved insiders. It sorts people. Like monograms, it has been used since the beginning of time as part of one's identity and incidentally for status among those in the "know". In our chosen field of work this system already existed.

The groups who sent workers to our area were coded locally by the Christian workers and were influenced by the abbreviated name of the group. They used catchy phrases like Pepsi Cola, Berry Jam, and Sea Bees. Information was shared with other individuals on a "need to know" criterion. This excluded many good Christians locally, even the pastors of the Union and Anglican Churches.

Code words were often identified with a logo, or some information known only to the initiated. The early Christians used the sign of the fish. When one met a person on the road, he might use the tip of his staff to make a crude drawing of a fish in the dust, during the course of the conversation. If it meant nothing to the other person, they exchanged news, and went on their way. If that other person took notice--and recognized it as a sign of Christian faith because he, too, was a believer -- he did the same. Then, the conversation might continue with an exchange of personal testimonies of how each came to know the Lord; comparing knowledge of Christians with whom they were acquainted and encouraging words for each other.

This kind of careful monitoring of others is necessary today in lands where enraged local persecution, followed by state prosecution, is likely. It was so in the early days of Christian growth and it is so today in some countries both Communist and Islamic where an opposing religious or political system prevails. Christians guard internal lines of security where external danger to persons and institutions exists. In more open societies Christians can be less protective. Signs of identity can be externalized.

The person who crosses himself may, by this sign, be asking God for protection from some expected evil, giving thanks for that protection, or asking God's blessing in some endeavor, strength or agility in some athletic feat. The reasons are endless. However, at the same time, he is communicating to the world, that it is the Christian God he is invoking. Wearing a cross, is another sign that many around the world recognize as Christian. The name Christian was bestowed in derision upon followers of Christ in Antioch of Syria. The same attitude happens still in vast areas of the world, where some kinds of pretense are camouflage, a basis of security.

Since our local codes underlined secretiveness some groups carried the charade further. They pretended to not know friends met on the street. Names, addresses and phone numbers were not written down. Even meetings were sometimes secretly held in a building. Each coming and leaving in singles or pairs at different times trying not to attract attention. "So and so works with Pepsi Cola," those in the know can say with a superior grin.. Such practices may make you feel safe. It can feel like fun and games but it is no way to witness or win sympathy for Christ the Messiah among the majority of people around you. Everyone was too busy maintaining his cover. Secrecy, unfortunately, always breeds suspicion. Suspicion promotes investigation and fear for national safety.

We Sea Bees came out immediately for reflecting what each group wanted and expected from us. For ourselves we gradually decided to be openly Christian but careful about what we printed and any reference to our sending body. We would not cross the line into what local police called Christian Propaganda, yet we would practice friendship evangelism on a person-to-person basis. We wondered if this would be difficult, but to the contrary many Muslims would say: "We accept your prophet why won't you accept ours?" We were surprised to learn people like to talk about religion, our problem was that we in the West are not used to talking about it. We were at a disadvantage. We had to learn apologetic strategies. How to defend our faith against attack.

But we also had another task; to encourage our fellow workers to become more public in their faith. By our dress and accent everyone knew we were outsiders, secular people were well known in higher technical and educational circles. But to meet a moral person from the West was considered unusual. Everyone saw our movies and knew what kind of people we were in our countries. But like people everywhere, holiness attracts their attention and admiration. There was the place to start rather than from secretiveness. We played the "pretend" game with the different groups, but I would talk of our witness opportunities. Once in an exchange of seminar papers on the local situation among the workers there, I did a paper on how to 'witness on a bus without a fuss'. Open a book and read silently a Christian book, Bible or tract in Turkish. People will read over your shoulder, looking away if you read too slowly and looking back when you turn the page. If they chose to read it's not your responsibility. No one will object, but some may ask where you can get the book or even if you are a Christian and what you are doing in their country. You had best have good answers prepared.

I could understand the fear of expulsion felt among the groups. It had happened a number of times to those selling literature door to door or those who passed out tracts. However, the police considered street work "Christian Propaganda". They arrested you and accompanied you to the bus or train station to deport you. The law allowed freedom, but as one friend said, "The police find it convenient to ignore laws they think ought not to exist".

To spend years learning the language and then be deported brought fear to the surface in all of us. But there were dodges to meet the threat. Some people got off the bus at the first stop and went back to town. If the police were too busy to wait with you, you could cash in your ticket and go home. You could take the next bus back to the city if they got you across the border, your name would not be on the black list on computer for several days. Other groups got set up to bring in summer young people to sell Christian books. Then if they were deported and didn't get off and away, they became automatic heroes on return to their home church.

I had some ways of dealing with the ultra-secretive. I had a joke that I used to loosen the fearful, hush-hush, nerves of those about me. "There was a volunteer with Berry Jam that was so covered that after three years no one knew that he was anything except a regular guy from the West." The bite in it was that it had almost happened in a few cases. Besides, I worked in an Islamic high school and everyone there knew and respected me as a Christian. We Sea Bees wore our faith on our sleeves so to speak and fearlessness is fortunately, contagious. We still didn't tell people we were missionaries, but most had already figured that out. The secrecy over the decade 1980-90 became less paranoid. As a national church grows and reaches out with national leaders the fear and suspicion lessens although the persecution continues.

If local people are outraged it is because some of their people are becoming Christians, not because they suspect converts and their teachers of being foreign spies. Let's not pretend, be an open, forthright Christian.

19

WATCH YOUR LANGUAGE

TURKISH IS A HARD LANGUAGE. I once watched an old veteran of the work show us how to translate a page of Christian material. The page filled with idiomatic phrases and current religious jargon was reduced to one paragraph of meaningful essence in our target language. Obviously they don't think like we do, nor talk with the same words translated into Turkish. Even the sentences and clauses are built opposite ours. Everything goes topsy-turvy. They translate from the start of our sentences, jump to the end and work back toward the front. Starting with the subject they skip to the object, then add the verb at the end. You cannot take the expressed words as containing the real meaning. The expression "I kiss your eyes", written in a Turkish letter is not a literal possibility; just as "I lost my head," is not actual in English.

There are other traps for the unaware as well. It was weeks before I realized that the first three lessons in our English book contained scandalous words in the Turkish language. I was teaching blasphemy: shameless sex words without any sense of wrong. I would ask the class to repeat the daily vocabulary after me. Most obeyed automatically. A minority reacted differently: a few made no sound at all; some had a silly grin on their faces; others exchanged knowing looks or giggled; more than one looked red faced and indignant. But I was an intensive teacher not waiting or watching for reactions. I was listening for phonetic reproduction. They had to get the sounds just right. I let them drill one by one up and down the rows. We had everyone repeat the dialogues with other students. Let me put most of the problem words into a few sentences. *'I am sick and tired of eating peaches. Anna*

Karanina is a long book. I'm pissed off because they pushed it. I feel sickish,

'These sentences contain nine sexually specific or dirty words, to Turkish ears. They might detect slight differences because of the English pronunciation but they would still hear words forbidden by their mamas. Prohibition, however, causes attraction. There seems to be a universal pleasure in saying some naughty words. 'Bitch' and 'bastard' come easy to most students, however the name of sexual parts seems to be more secret; to be shared with intimate friends only, if at all. Teachers soon learn to find many ingenious manners of evading the blunt use of these forbidden words. Contractions both negative and possessive will doctor and disguise verbs. Substitutes will take care of many of the nouns. But there is no state of complete freedom from the danger of embarrassment; especially when using a new language.

Language learning involves crossing many cultural boundaries. Dirty, sexy and body words occur in all languages. It's a universal fact. One language may use innocent words that in another has 'unmentionable' meanings. The same syllables convey approved or disapproved meanings. For example, the word spelled 'm-e-r-d' means virile, worthy, in Turkish but it's a 'four letter word' in French and means nothing in English. We were faced with difficulties even in calling the roll. I had a girl student named by a far seeing parent: Horizon = Üfük; others named Mumu and Satan. Numbers like eighty-one = seksen bir; eighty-four = seksen dirt; I hear you = Seni ishitim; the wharf = rektum. These innocent Turkish words suggest other meanings in English. I had difficulty in saying them at first. Learners are embarrassed to speak out anything prohibited in their own language.

In most languages verbs and nouns of the same syllables can mean different things. A pear, to appear; a peer, to peer; a pair, to pair off; to prepare, to pare potatoes. Other languages have the same kind of illogical, same sound but different meaning words. Hazel found that the noun 'task' or 'work' in Turkish has a different meaning: to urinate, if made into a verb. She was saved embarrassment by the class who realized, sympathized and covered up the mistake for her. After all, if you don't know, how can you avoid mistakes of this kind? Fortunately, teachers have prestige in Turkey.

Misunderstanding is always a two-way street. Listening in on a language you don't understand can produce moments of consternation.

Most languages will have funny or offensive sounding words for the unwary to stumble across. Good intentions are generally credited to the teacher but the offence is still conveyed until the new language begins to assume meaning and usefulness to the speaker. Some learners never get that far. Here too, a pattern appears.

It took only a few weeks to realize that some few students would immediately start to make excellent progress in language learning, well above the class average. The larger body of class members would form a central core and there would always be a few dropping out the bottom. They would stop attending or just survive as they fell behind. It wasn't always a matter of how they worked, attended or did homework. Teachers tried to make classes clear, easy and more fun. They work on attitudes and class morale. We could help some but always about the same percentage dropped out or excelled. The same situation existed among those learning Turkish.

People with an ear for music or a mind for math seemed to do better. Africans who were accustomed to hear and speak three or four languages in their early environment were phenomenal in their learning ability. Europeans did well. English speakers were generally among the worst. Yet on the other hand English could be poorly spoken with accents, yet be understood by those used to it. Turks, like the French, have a hard time understanding without phonetic precision in those speaking their language.

Once the teacher or the student is well into the material and understands both languages he becomes extremely useful. There are better paying jobs awaiting those who excel. We eventually moved to Marmara University. The students went to business, tourism, banking or government. Promotion and money went with western languages, we never lacked students yet we were always speaking English, their target language, not Turkish our target language. However, our visa depended on our teaching.

Turkish at the turn of the century was a language that had taken the Arabic alphabet and important religious and business words from that source into their own. They also had incorporated many Persian words into their vocabulary. In 1928 Ataturk changed the alphabet to a Latin form and ordered the research of old words of Turkish origin. They created new words for the teaching of modern science and education. In fifty years they moved as far as English had from the time of King James.

Some of Ataturk's early speeches are nearly incomprehensible to modern school children. Grandparents cannot understand their grandchildren's science books. The generation gaps are large and troublesome in Turkey.

Social position and politics are reflected in vocabulary and grammar changes. This means they have several ways of expressing the same thoughts: with or without old Arabic words. The use of Arabic words is frowned on. However, if you don't know the more common ones, you fail to understand part of the population. This means learning a double vocabulary. It also meant that Bible translation was an important part of the work carried on by evangelical groups. Actually three New Testaments were underway in our time: one by Bible Society; one by an Evangelical Association; one by the Roman Catholic Church. Each was different enough to appeal to various segments of the population, but all were saying the same message in different vocabularies.

I found myself seeking opportunities to better our Turkish but failed to discover any way to speed that goal. It took us four years to get where others were in two years of language study. However, being a sought after top-notch English teacher brought opportunities to witness to the aspiring youth and other teachers. Opportunities for friendship were frequent.

Other 'expatriates' were out learning by the 'bare foot' language system, espoused by many linguists. Their contacts were storekeepers and street acquaintances that they visited, a scheduled minimum of six hours or fifty persons on the streets each day. They had to leave every few months to return with a temporary tourist visa. They learned Turkish much faster, but with slang, 'street' language, regional accents and bad grammar often included. Not all of us were able to handle that kind of situation. We were working for the same purpose and attending the same churches but were befriending different kinds of people.

The diversity of home countries among expatriates made for an international body and created an attractive atmosphere in the English speaking churches. Most churches created a Turkish youth meeting as adjunct to the English congregation. We modeled Christian's social and spiritual lives together. Young people excused their attendance to their parents as learning language or meeting international people. Some students came for a while to satisfy their curiosity. Others came for friends. Others came for deep needs and some found Christ as Lord and Savior. It was rarely a fast process. Struggles within and without were characteristic. The road to heaven is narrow, steep and full of obstacles. The miracle is that there is a small but steady flow of converts in an environment usually indifferent, if not hostile, to the Gospel.

The government, conscript army, media and general population are against any beliefs that remain outside the accepted values of the state. The differences between Ataturk secularism and Islam they are prepared to accept but Protestant Christianity, which some admire, is inadmissible to the social body. The result can only be prosecution in legal matters and persecution by all segments of the society. There is no freedom of proclamation or public witness allowed in this society's beloved language, no matter how well you speak it. This antipathy is, for the moment, stronger than the inexorable cultural pull toward Europe and the West in general. But a Turkish Protestant Church was hardly known before in their history. They know little about it and fear it, they are ignorant of its long-range good purposes and bottom lines and political effects, because politics and religion are inseparable in their minds. Remember, very few have ever heard the gospel:that Jesus loves and saves those who come to Him. Converts do speak a Modern Turkish the young understand and find attractive. By law only Turkish citizens can become pastors of Turkish churches. So the future of the churches rests on a tiny group of very brave men who are sifted severely. Their eloquence is founded in the Spirit and the Word, in a language worth listening to.

I spoke of things I did not understand,
things too wonderful for me to know.
Job 42:3

20

ABRAM LIVED IN TENTS

THE BIBLICAL ANCESTORS WERE RESTLESS and lived in tents, moving frequently. Our life for God has many of the same qualities, including tents. But Hazel hates them! That and sand between the toes; sparks in the face; salt water dried on sunburned skin; insects in food: in short (or long if you want more of a list) lots of things associated with tents. But summer camp came up every year, and often, it was our privilege to attend.

Marshall, who believes that 'into each life some rain must fall', takes the stoic's position. He gladly suffers on! "Enjoy it while it lasts; it too, will soon pass." But Hazel says: "Look at the condition it leaves you in after all that suffering. And think how long it takes to get your parts back like they were before the madness struck and you took to tents."

Interestingly, Turks love being at one with nature and the summer excursion into beach and mountains is a national passion. They, too, had ancestors who resided in tents or rather yurts, a felt tent with a willow frame to hold its sides up in a circle. They, too, long for the restless days of old when they followed the herds in the northern steppes and lived adventurously. That is to say, from hand to mouth. There may be a touch of masochism or is it sadism in their system? You know: I'll show everyone how I can take it, (as long as you do too.) Togetherness, "ber-a-ber-lik", is a constant theme in all their actions.

A camp, to be really adventurous, cannot be too near any village stores or other places of convenient commerce. It must be located in the outback, distantly connected by rutted trail, or broken road. Telephones would ruin the whole outing. Latrines are dug and sheeting is hung around flimsy poles to give the illusion of privacy. Primitive is the key word here and the more the better.

The schedule began with an early, kick-start prayer meeting at dawn, before breakfast. Everybody was invited (except for the breakfast crew) but it was the "faithful few" who usually came. Next was breakfast. The enormous steaming cups of hot tea gave you a wonderful start. Add the white goat cheese, soft black olives, and slabs of fresh baked bread (delivered by some local entrepreneur), which you could slather with jelly from a bowl on the table. Most mornings there were oranges. The list of names on the cleanup crew was posted and all others scattered to get ready for the day's activities.

Bible study for the grown-ups, and Daily Vacation Bible School for the kids was next. Usually, we sang and the Scripture was read aloud to the large group for the introduction. Then there was one teacher for the women, with another for the men and several for the youth (with girls in one and boys in the other or a mix depending on teacher and subject). All the study teachers were respected leaders who prepared well ahead of time. They tried to keep the size of the groups down, so that everyone could take part and ask questions if they wished.

Then came swim time. They always chose a place where water was near by. A walk of over 15 minutes was considered a hardship in the blazing sun. On the last day of the camp they would need it for a baptismal service, too. The seashore was preferred for sunbathing.

Swimming lasted up to lunchtime. No one wanted to be late for that. The exercise made everybody hungry. You would be amazed at the great meals the ladies turned out with the primitive means of cooking. They had few leftovers and many satisfied and sleepy campers. Lunch needed another crew for cleanup. After the first day all the crews had names and rallied to finish the job best and fastest.

In the afternoons, everyone was free to take part in a variety of activities as they wished. The young kids were usually put down for a nap. The mothers and grandmothers did their handwork (knitting, crocheting, netting, embroidering, etc.). The weary napped. The courts were favorite places for the youth groups. If there were other campers nearby, they were invited to organize volleyball or "futbol" (soccer) teams. The competition grew quite fierce over the two weeks.

About four in the afternoon everyone was served a snack. Neighboring campers who had come to play the games, or watch the skit were included. Some of the adults, invited other adults over for a cup of tea. Many who had seen us attending their church services since February (of that first year), had never had time to get acquainted with us before. The ladies had done some baking before they came, and so treated us to their best cooking, and took this as an opportunity to find out WHO we were and WHAT we had come to Turkey for. We formed some lovely friendships that lasted all those years that we stayed.

Like the Maritimers of Canada, those matriarchs revealed to us who their sisters and brothers, children, grandchildren, and whole extended families were. (I say "matriarchs", because the "patriarchs" were back in town making a living, and could only come out for a weekend.) They felt so sorry for us so far away from our kith and kin. They invited us to their homes back in Istanbul, and at subsequent services, made a point to greet us, chat profusely and present us to the members of the family who had not been able to join us at camp.

One widow that we had already met was especially friendly. She had a beautiful crown of white hair, and boarded a number of the young single Christian workers in her home. She knew only a few words of English. She always greeted everyone with the words," Jesus is coming soon!" She had a husband and daughter waiting for her in Heaven, and sounded like she could hardly wait to join them. She occupied a folding chair that someone had brought, and someone brought her tea to her, and she "received" a small crowd around her as though she were a queen. After a few years, I was shocked to learn that she was the very same age as I was! I was running around directing games while she sedately looked on.

Always, while the camp was on, some local authorities came by one afternoon to "give a welcome" and register everyone who came to the camp. If the person registered was a minor and his father had a Muslim name, the parents were always notified. Of course, many times it was the FATHER who was registering them there. Most of the Christians attending the camp were minorities: Greek, Armenian, Syrian, Kurds, and even a few Jews.

Later in the day Hazel organized some games, like going on "Paul's Missionary Journeys", "The Wilderness Wanderings", or "In the Footsteps of Jesus", involving everyone interested. Alternate days, there were sometimes skits from Bible Stories, or ones that would teach some Bible truth. Those visiting teams, and other neighboring campers, were invited to these afternoon fun times, and also to the evening song and preaching services.

Another swim time and then, about dark, supper came. There was a little time to clean up and get ready for the evening service. There was a big hymn sing, and lots of special music. Everyone who played an instrument brought it and played, even the electronic ones! Since we needed a generator to light up the meeting, they had amplifiers and everything that could be plugged in. People shared their hymnbooks and Bibles with their visiting neighbors. Some people, curious about Christianity, found this a non- threatening way to learn what the Christians really believe. Some stayed to question, argue, and generally investigate further. A few fervent Muslims thought they might convert the preacher, then the debate would go on until late. The youth would stay up all hours to listen and it was always done calmly by both sides. Anger rarely flared.

There was a nightcap of some hot tea or milk, supervised by a crew, and then off to visit or to bed. Turks are night owls, so visits continued till curfew. We went three successive years to the Aegean Sea near the border. Each year was memorable but the location had to change after that because nearby authorities became worried by the interest and enthusiasm aroused by the presence of these nice Christians. They refused permission to camp there again. By the next summer someone came up with another area where they could get permission to camp. Camping, while rough was bearable even for Hazel. She sang an old song that goes: "if we suffer for Him here, we will reign with Him there."

21

A TASTE OF TURKEY

Turkish delight was a product of the opulent Ottoman Empire, a refinement of taste and sweetness to corrupt even the likes of fault-finding Edmund in C. S. Lewis' book: The Lion, the Witch and the Wardrobe. Turkish sweets are all of the same attractive nature whether it's *baclava, pishmania, sheker pare, kurabiye, helva, or flan* with caramel sauce. Death by sweets is a definite possibility in Turkey.

Turkish food is acclaimed by many world travelers as one of the best. We agree with such judgments and are going to give you some of the reasons why we like the taste of Turkey.

Breakfast may seem skimpy if you're not fond of soup; in eastern Turkey they serve cream of wheat as well, and call it soup. Black olives, white feta cheese and bread are the normal breakfast, with jam or jelly for the bread if you prefer. Butter? It's extra. Scalding sweet tea is served in a cup! At any other time of day it's served in a small glass.

Tea is served every hour of the day in a small tulip shaped glass as a social event. It is also brought by special tea boys to the offices during the work hours, morning and afternoon. Shops serve potential customers this beverage while you wait, chat or bargain. It is brought from a teahouse that produces only this product by contract to the local stores. The business buys a 100 - 500 or more tokens, based on how many clients they expect to have that month. Then, as the tea glasses are picked up at the end of the day, there is a token with each of them. This saves the trouble of looking for change every time you want a glass of tea. Restaurents do not serve tea. If you want tea with or after your meal, they send someone from the nearest tea house. They will not give you a tea bag. They send to to the nearest tea house and it is delivered. The boys who deliver the tea have a special round tray that looks like the apparatus for hanging plants. It's topped by a ring that the boy holds, so that it naturally stays level and doesn't spill the tea. A saucer with two sugar cubes and a "teaspoon" (the size of our demitasse coffee spoons) sits on top of the tiny glass so that the tea remains hot and you have everything right there. As the delivery boy makes his way through the crowds that always throng the streets of the city, his movements are as fluid as a ballet dancer, but as rapid and purposeful as a quarterback dodging through the opposing defense players on the way to a touchdown.

At noon we would usually eat a pancake sized pizza called a *lahmacun* (pronounced lah-mah-june), *doner* (small pieces of beef, lamb, or chicken shaved from a huge cone of meat served with lettuce and tomato, on a hamburger type bun), or a grilled cheese sandwich.

If you got hungry before mealtime -- crisp sesame seed rolls called *semit* were just right. The bread part was the thickness of a bagel, but the hole in the middle was 4 inches across. The vendor, called a *semitgee*, had very little invested -- he came out at mid-morning with a cane held vertically with maybe 20 of those tasty treats hanging from it. Others had what looked like a popcorn machine mounted on wheels so they could set up near the bus stops where hundreds of people passed, getting off one bus and onto another, at every hour all day long. Another interesting fact about the *semit* vendor was his ability to make change. You could never get change from the bank: they just dealt in BIG BILLS! If you needed change for bus fare or a phone token, ask the "semitgee"!

Shish kabobs were readily available and very tasty. Anybody with a small barbecue could sell them. *Shish* means sword and this food originated with soldiers in the field. Somebody would kill a rabbit and they would chop the meat up into chunks and skewer it onto their swords to cook over an open fire. Now you can buy wooden (disposable) skewers or metal (recyclable) ones. Walking by the harbor one day, we also discovered fish kabobs, and enjoyed them. The barbecue sat on the middle seat of a small motorboat, the vendors standing on either side of it. The one nearest the pier took the orders, and delivered them to the customer, while the other slid the fish into a bun along with a chopped mixture of lettuce, tomatoes and onion.

Sweets consisted of many types of cakes, cookies, and *baklava* drowned in honey or sugar syrup. There is one that looks like shredded wheat, but made in a 16" or 24" round pan with many variations of nuts and fruit. At one special season of the year it is served with cheese inside: hot and melted. It is a personal favorite. 'Skek-err pah-'ray is a cookie that is soaked. A short bread with a long name, called ah-gee-bah-dem koor-rah-bee-yay, is just one of the many nice dry almond cookies. *Helva* is like very sweet, cold, cream of wheat that can be sliced like cake., when made at home. In commercial quantities, bought at the bakery, it tastes like sweet sand and comes in many flavors and colors. Remembering back, my mouth just waters!

Flan, with caramelized sugar like our custard, is very popular and there was one business where nothing but puddings were sold. There again you found a great variety of far too sweet desserts were served. If only the world was as sweet as our taste.

We enjoyed all these things, it was fast food all day in the city and the dinning out was fabulous at night. The evening meal was always served very late. The *meze* (appetizers) alone were too numerous to count and for us several were worthy of being the whole meal. We weren't used to the fantastic variety and high prices. Quality costs.

At the end of a trip around the Seven Churches of the Revelation, one of our Canadian visitors took us out to a meal at a classy restaurant on the Bosphorus. He included our guide and his family—a party of eight. We ordered ONLY "meze": 12 different varieties. There were Jumbo shrimp some stuffed and others fried, miniature cocktail shrimp with small pide bread chips: various stuffed vegetables: tomatoes, zucchini, sweet peppers, eggplant, as well as cabbage and grape leaves that they prefer to call—wraps. Pureed smoked eggplant and *humus*, made from chickpeas are served with little finger food tidbits made of paper-thin bread.

This bread (called philo dough in Canada and US) is the basis for many dishes. Sometimes it is folded in half, it's edges sealed and baked. It blows up like a balloon, and is brought just after you have ordered, to occupy you until the rest of your meal is ready. Sometimes half it's 30" diameter circle is slathered with some savoury filling; folded over, covered with another filling; and then rolled like we roll a jelly roll. This roll is then coiled into a 30" pan and spiraled using one roll after another until it fills the pan. While it was flat, it was spread with a savoury, cheesy, or sweet mixture. Other times it was stacked eight or ten deep, again with one of those fillings between each layer. Many women made their own dough, but it was possible to buy the sheets already made at the market, by the kilo. There were several of those tidbits among our *meze*. What a marvelous meal that was. We all ate until we couldn't! I'm sure that none of us will ever forget that "appreciation" meal.

The best food came to our home and those of friends when we met together to enjoy the best basic nutrition in the best of company under the best of causes.

Marshall came home from the hospital after a knee operation, and his friend came to visit him. This older Turkish teacher of English that we sometimes helped to prepare his lessons, ordered his wife to make *manta* for Marshall. *Manta* is a pasta dish made from 2" squares of pasta, with a teaspoonful of meat filling. It looks like coins tied in a hankie, and a batch is at least 100 of these(it tastes like ravioli). It's only made on very special occasions. But we were treated to it numerous times during our 15 years there.

Hospitality is a virtue Mohammed encouraged. *Misafirlik*, is their word for the entertaining of guests. It establishes a bond of confidence. We are told of a Great Banquet called the marriage supper of the Lamb in the Gospel. That will clearly be a feast to remember with friends and family combined with the great ones of God's kingdom present with us.

Most of us live junk food lives. Books, magazines and T.V. give us an endless parade of "mind-fill" of questionable value. We need to be selective in feeding our souls, if we intend to enjoy a healthy life: mind, body and soul. This has always been true. Philippians 4:8 KJV gives us some guide lines: "Whatsoever things are TRUE, whatsoever things are HONEST, whatsoever things are JUST, whatsoever things are PURE, whatsoever things are LOVELY, whatsoever things are of GOOD REPORT; if there be any VIRTUE, if there be any PRAISE, THINK ON THESE THINGS!"

*See, I have placed before you an open door
that no one can shut.*
Revelation 3:8

How the gold has lost its luster,
the fine gold become dull!
Lamintations 4:1

22

INFERNAL INFLATION

WE HAD BEEN MILLIONAIRES TWICE in our lives, we certainly didn't want to be one again. Everyone supposes a luxurious life style would characterize such a status, but in much of the third world everyone who expects to survive holds that amount or more. Where everyone can be a millionaire no one is happy, it shows a society in collapse. The million is in local currency and may represent only a small amount in American or Canadian dollars. As local money devaluates the middle class is thinned, pensions lose all significance and both the old and the struggling poor fall out of the picture. But the process is painfully slow, filled with daily struggles as workers try to gain more to compensate for the increase in prices. The businessman struggles to get more for his product because of the increased cost of raw material and labor. The producers are bound by the cost of energy and labor. Machinery is more expensive than farm produce, which keeps the farmer down. Debt mounts and government taxation becomes draconian. People in distress are hard to govern, making security more important. Army and police grow in size and power. Government puts more faith in discipline and order than in the slower processes of democracy and free expression. Real estate and gold climb in value and everyone buys on time for those foolish enough to give it. Neither government nor people are willing to bite the bullet and reverse the process. Spending to the limit is the order of the day: money seeks to rescue itself by publishing more and higher numbers on the paper bills. Sound familiar?

Our first hosts' home was enormous -- only six rooms, but big enough to divide so that it seemed to be ten ample rooms. They were paying 3,500 TL (Turkish Lira), which at the time they moved in was worth about U. S. One hundred dollars. But after several years of inflation had diminished to about US$ 53. They assured us we would have to pay more. It turned out to be about three times more. When the inflation continued to worsen, the government passed a new law that the renter would have to pay an increase in rent of 40% a year. The army coup in 1980 smashed the violent actions of the political parties and set up martial law by suspending all constitutional rights. They filled both graveyards and jails. Without the right of appeal, justice was without recourse. Injustices occurred. The army stopped the terrorists by the application of greater violence. The Ataturk way, a policy and philosophy 50 years old, returned to power. General Evren (the name means Universe), head of the army, promised peace and imposed it. They crushed the leftist's parties, and outlawed some of them. They did less damage to the rightist parties and people soon suffered a revival of religious fanaticism.

About the same time world banks from Tokyo to London and New York decided that Turkey was a profitable place to be represented now that peace had come. They leased villas with a view of the Bospherus. Since we could not pay 1 to 3 thousand dollars a month rent we did not compete directly; but their presence, paying in US currency, forced the whole rent market up and out of sight.

In a twelve-year period we lived successively in three different houses on the European side of the city followed by three different houses on the Asian side of Istanbul. The second house in each case was only a matter of a few months. However, we had friends to aid in their search for shelter. We kept a constant eye open for housing, exchanging information with friends, it was a part of conversation. We paid 160 dollars for the first place and when inflation reduced the value to 100 dollars we started paying the 40% increase to try to keep the original evaluation. We paid $400 for our last, brand new apartment, which was monthly a million lira. We were now millionaires on a teacher's wages but my salary at the University was only equal to U.S. $500. We found this situation hard to live in. Transport and food took double the remainder. We had to draw from our home bank.

The country was up for sale. Investments flooded in. The price of buying into factories and businesses desperate for hard cash was a bonanza for financiers. Money for new improvements and building was available. Government and private debt climbed, affecting everything. Money became more important than family honor, loyalty or religion. Government resistance to the Turkish Protestant Churches became less by reason of distraction. We Christians, were law abiding, many others were not. There was no freedom of proclamation, but we felt almost free. For the moment we were free from harassment.

Politicians pursued popularity and the people and government opposed any concessions to Greece in Cyprus or to the Kurds as a linguistic and religious minority. As a result the Greeks opposed Turkish entrance into the European Market. A Kurdest terrorist organization grew and became active at this time. The collapse of the Soviet Union brought more changes. The Turkish government determined to help the newly liberated Turkish republics in central Asia. Army Expenditure and investments in the new republics took their toll in high taxation and huge borrowing. In the twelve years we lived in the country, inflation ate up the value of their money. Maintenance tired them. Loans tempted them to venture more. Extravagance ruined them.

When we left the country in 1991 a million Lira was considered average to rent a two-bedroom apartment for a month. Our first year it was only nine thousand. Twenty years after our first arrival in Turkey I landed in 1999 at the airport, put my bankcard in the automatic teller machine for exchange, I took the lowest choice and got one bill worth 5 million Turkish Lira. My home bank marked its value as fourteen dollars. I bought a gift worth nearly a million from a florist for my host of one night. I wondered if a million were enough for the grandson to deliver packages and letters to friends scattered across the city. One becomes disoriented as to costs and value unless you are living where the action is occurring. Governmental policies fan infernal inflation and furnishes a sense of bewilderment and timidity in individuals and the general population. Gain cannot equal the loss of value.

In the presence of God our earthly gain, though great, is likewise minimal; our goods and social position will count for little. Investments in what Jesus recommends will be of true value and carry an eternal credit. In God's kingdom, the poor may become rich while the rich remain poor. Much depends on how you use your strength, time and goods. Your faith, or lack of the same, will govern your spirit and actions. Dividends and rewards are received on the basis of this faith and action.

God turns the tables on all of us: the one who now has little gets much; the one who has much gets little and the first are last! Where do you stand in this?

The Lord gave and the Lord has taken away; may the name of the Lord be praised.
Job 1:21

23

MANY, MANY MINIBUSES

In cities with multimillion populations, transport is a chief and vital concern for everyone. Each main street in Istanbul has its share of minibuses. Some had trolleys, which were supplanted by buses and then reintroduced for the tourists. The addition of hydrofoils to supplement the ferries and newer two story buses plus hinged double machines simply add to the horrendous traffic.

Turkey in Europe is small, only the city of Edirne buffers it near the borders of Greece and Bulgaria; ancient and dangerous rivals. The West Side of the city has to be free for defensive maneuvering. Industries are safe to the East, out of harm's way. As the suburbs grow the trek to the center of the city becomes longer and more wearisome.

The towns and villages extend eastward for over a hundred kilometers. Fast commuter trains connect them like beads on a rosary. Ferries leave regularly for central Istanbul but with all this it can still take from one to two hours, one-way. Two teachers from the same centrally located school decided to have their wives meet with them in the older man's home. It took them two and a half hours to arrive across town. They enjoyed the meal but never did it again.

Even Sunday morning, the lightest time of the week, it is a long trip to church and longer on the return. We went for the day and usually ate lunch with some of the worshipers down town. Believers came in groups to the many cafeterias. Some favored one place, some another but becoming regular they would bear witness, give tracts or invite some of the personnel to special events at church.

Church, for us, was a multiple affair: English at 9:30 (also at 11:) Turkish at 11:00 elsewhere and sometimes afternoon meetings at a third place. Sometimes we had night meetings too. When the Dutch Chapel choir sang or gave a special concert somewhere we would get home near 11PM. The buses stopped working about 9 to 10 p.m. as did the Tunel (subway). The ferries worked till after midnight and the minibuses worked all night, but with less frequency. We never found an hour that a minibus was not available. They always had enough passengers to make a profit, although at the price you wonder how.

Each minibus follows a regular route from which it will not vary; yet it will stop anywhere in any block to take on or drop passengers. The buses had marked stops, but not the minibus. They race madly along filling the city with noise and the passengers with fear as they abruptly pull to a stop to pick up or drop people along the way, then accelerate to top speed. One long wide street is called the Minibus Road. Bagdad, the other road, much used by them, is parallel and close to the shore. Bagdad has the more fashionable shops and eating-places. The parks and high rises are beautiful and expensive. Many foreign business people live along the Marmara seashore. The Minibus Road comes after the Shore Road, Bagdad, and the railroad. It services the poorer areas before arriving at the highway to Bursa, Ankara the capitol and interior Turkey. We lived near the Minibus road, as did most of our friends. Marmara University faced the same road. It was our daily friend and artery of travel. Some depended on the urban trains for fast service, but the road held our allegiance.

Tom and Gladys lived for a time, in an apartment behind a gas station, a half block from the Minibus Road. Young people passing in the night could see the living-room light; and if it was still on, call a stop and go visit. Gladys, who hated noise and claimed to turn into a pumpkin after 10 PM, graciously fed and cared for them until they left, satisfied in body and soul, much later in the night.

Calling a stop is a literal truth, you shout, `Inejek var,` (if you intend to get off) or `Dur` (stop) if he, unheeding, is passing the corner you had called. Timing is of the utmost importance, if your feet hurt or you have packages to carry. You dare not doze on the minibus. During Ramazan, when the men fast by day and eat by night; the dozing passenger is a common occurrence and most try to be home by dark to eat the first meal since dawn.

Perhaps I have made riding the minibus sound very easy, it isn't. You have to stand in line to get loaded at the docks. You wait your turn while the minibuses pull up and load to the last seat and pull out. The line, reduced by between 12 or 20 passengers, continues to grow at the end as people rush out of the ferries to seek their bus or minibus connection. Some change vehicles or mode of transit, again, further away from the city. If you wait along the road they will only stop if they have room. But each driver is responsible for filling his vehicle, more people = more money, and you can stand, holding on for dear life. At rush hour the minibus road is crowded with every kind of private and commercial mobility. There are few traffic lights so pedestrians crossing the street is a major challenge: requiring bravery, alertness and a good sense of timing. However, a woman with a baby carriage is ahoother story. She looks for an opening, and strolls leisurely across while buses and cars screech to a halt. Hazel believes that mothers teach their babies bravery in the face of danger this way.

If your group is large enough you can take a taxi, spelled *taksi*, and for five persons you average the same price all would pay on a bus. We did this frequently when we were with friends or visitors. You can also rent a minibus to meet a crowd at the airport or to carry luggage. In a *taksi* make sure you are in one that has a meter or you could be over charged. There is a different rate for after midnight. The driver usually took off before you were well settled and expected to get instructions as you speed toward your destination-not an easy task when your language ability is slow or the directions to a friend's house difficult. If two or three persons join in to help explain, the ride becomes precarious as he dodges between cars and asks questions about your destination at the same time. One or another is forced to remain silent and pray while the other explains again. Once in such a situation Marshall turned to Hazel and said sweetly: "Hazel dear, would you please help me?" "Of course." she responded eagerly. He responded pleasantly, "Shut up." Friends gasped, a lady passenger suppressed a giggle. But Hazel sat quietly, to the admiration of all, while Marshall went over the instructions again and the cabby nodded and concentrated on his driving.

One night Marshall was coming home with Hazel late at night and on leaving the minibus discovered he had left his briefcase. The driver was speeding out of sight. He thought of all the trouble that would involve: looking up the office, describing the driver, the hour, the line, etc. and looked around for another minibus. One drew up at that moment and he hopped aboard and as he paid, described his plight to the driver. With a look of glee the driver assured him they would catch the minibus. He would stop to let off passengers but so did the other driver and they caught them in about two kilometers. As they pulled along side them, Marshall signaled, everybody signaled, with all the other passengers cheering; his little bus pulled ahead of the one with the briefcase to stop. They recognized him, stopped, and one of the riders held up Marshall's briefcase. The chasing minibus rushed on ahead with a triumphant honking of horns (they boast several!) and waving of hands. Marshall gladly retrieved his property to the congratulations of the other passengers and waved a thankful farewell as they zoomed away. He now had to cross the road and catch another minibus back to our corner and home to Bora Apartment. Life on the minibus road had its dramatic moments.

It's easy to despair when life gets crowded and circumstances work against you. Prompt action will be the answer to some problems and prompt prayer to others.

"But never despair,
it will get you nowhere.
Act with your mind,
let your heart be in prayer."

God makes almost everything relative and solvable. It's a learning process with God as the teacher; so keep hope alive, be patient and seek His answer.

24

A SHELTER FROM THE STORM

As wayfarers in the world we attended camp each summer, the campsite was near the Greek border where we would go to renew our visa. We were immersed in the language and found opportunity to understand the people we came to serve. It was a time of integration into a lovely community of believers composed of many nations and languages. The fortnight was well spent, exhausting and exhilarating.

The third year at camp, we were assigned an inner tent meant to be a bedchamber. It should have been covered by a much larger heavier canvas one. It was designed to stay up by tying it to the under side of the big enveloping one - almost like a mosquito net. But we had no outer envelope, tent or otherwise, and the flimsy thing was put off to one side of the grounds to give us privacy: almost as if we were newly wed! In our late-fifties, we felt it a nice, but unnecessary gesture. We had invested in an arctic sleeping bag. That really means two mummy-shaped down-filled bags. Hazel took the inner, smaller one, and Marshall had the larger one. There was room for our two suitcases, with one of the sleeping bags stretched across them at night and we could almost stand straight up inside the tent. It must have measured 72"(183cm)square,& 60"(153cm) high. They secured it to the branches in a cluster of several small trees, with strong ties at the tent's four corners. It sagged.

Most of the families had brought a small stove (in order to serve a personal cup of tea between the common meals for everybody), all the games for the kids, some handwork for the restful moments, reading material, lawn chairs, and all the swimming gear. Many had their own tents. The singles and the other families stayed in army tents, bought from some North American surplus store, and had been acquired over the years.

Everybody had duties: the men pitched the tents, set up the kitchen, hauled the water, dug the latrines and trash pits (several during the fifteen day camp), marked off the courts, and put up the nets for games. The women fixed meals, washed the clothes, minded the children, and bargained for the fresh produce that the local farmers came to offer for the feeding of this multitude. The preparation of and cleanup after meals involved EVERYBODY: men, women and children. They had enough people to make about five teams--that way you only had to do one cleanup each day, and it rotated from one meal to another as well.

We didn't have enough language to lead a Bible study, or the singing, so we mostly observed, and took part when possible. Our friend who had been designated to provide some games for the young people at our first camp, was not sure he would be able to be there, since his wife was expecting a baby just any minute. He asked if we could substitute for him. We said that if others would manage the direction, we would do the preparations. We took markers, poster board, and such and worked on several games. One turned out to be quite popular, and after that first year (a tour of *Biblical Sites in Turkey*), we had to come up with a new tour each year: Isreal's *Wilderness Wanderings, In the Steps of Jesus and St. Paul's Missionary Journeys*, to name a few.

During the camp setup, Hazel's job was numbering the tents. There was a general control sheet that had a space to record the key person in each tent. Often it was the mother of the family, since some of the Dads worked during the week and only came out for weekends. One was named from each tent for singles. There were 44 tents. It was like a buzzing little village.

There were friends from our churches, (we went to a minimum of two each Sunday all our years in Turkey). Both included English speaking and Turkish friends. Then there were some new people from the other congregations in Istanbul and visitors from Ankara, Adana and Izmir.

We got to know each other during the first ten days of the two weeks, three Sundays, of camp. Then came the storm. Those who had a radio mentioned that a big blow was expected that night. It had already hit Istanbul, and was traveling west toward where we were camping on the Aegean Sea. Everything was fine when we went to bed, and were off to a deep sleep after a busy day.

Marshall was in his sleeping bag on top of the two suitcases. Hazel's was on the other (soft) side of the tent. The water began to seep into her sleeping bag through the fabric floor. It also began to drip from the center of the square top of the tent. Hazel tried to find something that she could push up the center with. She wanted to drain the top down the side now it sagged like a basin. Wakened suddenly, Marshall told her to get back into her sleeping bag so it wouldn't get her wet. He was feeling groggy, being startled out of a sound sleep. She protested that she was already wet -- and she got that way IN HER SLEEPING BAG!

While she was hunched, almost standing, braced against the side, pushing a broom against the top; the water was streaming down the side and under the tent. Marshall stood up in his dry bed to help hold the broom. Each time the square top got pushed above the edge level a new splash and spill occurred. Marshall joked about getting wet, but Hazel was past humor, she was shivering, absolutely drenched. He shut up and held the broom alone, as the best way to serve. It was, after all, his turn to get wet.

Soon someone came to see if we were OK. Seems four tents had immediately collapsed, and their occupants had had to move in with other people. They could see that our tent was still hanging there, but they wondered if we were afraid of the lightning and wind and wanted to move out as well. We could hear the people praying and calling upon God to spare them.

We opted to stay where we were, and Hazel managed to sneak out a towel from inside of the suitcase, dry off somewhat, and then crowded into Marshall's sleeping bag. That was really close quarters!

The rain became gentle after what seemed like a long time. The thunder, lightning and wind passed on.

After the storm had passed we got a little sleep, and woke up to an absolutely brilliant sunshiny morning, with everything washed ever so clean! In all, 10 tents of the 44 fell during that night, and EVERYONE had been very crowded. The rest of the camp time, there were wet things strung along every tent rope, guy wire, and other lines were stretched between trees. Suitcases were emptied and put out open to the hot sun. Some vital documents and pictures that we carried in Hazel's train case were soaked --one being her passport-- and had to be watched while they were drying.

The news from the city was that some men set out in a rowboat to cross the Bosphorus because there was an emergency and the ferries were not running. The boat was capsized and though they found one man, the others were never seen again. There were no casualties in our camp, so there was a great prayer of thanksgiving that went up that day.

When the camp ended, there were still a few things that had to be packed wet. I said there were no casualties, but Hazel did lose her voice. She was several months recovering it. There were other results.

Some workers had brought some converts who had been on drugs. Some were going through the depressions and longings associated with withdrawal. In English we call it "cold turkey", it is a time of difficulty. Neighbors heard about their presence, perhaps old associates saw them or they testified to someone. Interest was high but negative on the part of most permanent residents and visitors alike. They, like people here, fear victims who are hooked on the drug habit. After all, Turkey has legal and illegal production of drugs; both opium and pot. Many foreigners and locals practicing or seeking the use of drugs fill the daily scene. It was a part of our ministry there. It is difficult to watch the agonies of withdrawal symptoms at work in both young and old. Cold Turkey is a dread reality. It was the last year we were allowed to hold camp in that community.

The rest of the evening services, that last week, were filled with the testimonies of some of those Christians who, during the storm, had made some vow to the Lord; if he would spare their lives. Others made a decision to follow Christ if He would save them. Even a few of those neighboring campers decided the time had come to make things right with God.

Though not all those who made decisions were baptized on that last day, but many were, and it was a beautiful service under the Aegean sun, as each committed himself through Jesus to God.

Storms seem to be a necessary ingredient in human life. We never seek Him otherwise. We need to realize our helplessness and dependence on God. Storms make us aware that our lives are often not pleasing to Him and sometimes displeasing to us or our families as well. Their fury and power become realities to measure ourselves against. We are not complete masters of our world, there are mightier forces at work around us.

We never went to a full two week stay at another camp but we were in Turkey long enough to see many of the troubled young people straighten out and find salvation in Jesus at a camp and grow into happy, healthy, responsible adults; marrying and raising their children "in the admonition of the Lord."

Many waters cannot quench love;
rivers cannot wash it away.
Song of Songs 8:7

But where can wisdom be found? Where does understanding dwell? Man does not comprehend its worth.
Job 28:12, 13a

25

U. LEARN IT!

My friend Howard was teaching English at Marmara University. It is named for the Marble Sea to the south of the city. This university dominates education on the Asian side of the metropolitan area. The eastern side of the Bosphorus straits had always been subservient to Istanbul on the western side. It served as a quiet bedroom adjunct to the more than two thousand year old center of commerce, government and education. Roberts College was there on the northwest of the Bospherous strait in Europe. The Technical and Sultan's colleges are there too, in downtown Istanbul. However, with the new development of the industrial areas, the eastern towns: Uskadar, Kadikoy, Erenkoy and Bostanca in Asia, grew to new importance.

Marmara was the newest of the Universities and located on the Asian side. At Erenkoy between two of the larger centers the University developed. They were still constructing buildings when we were there. Some of our classes were in barracks put up as temporary classrooms. Workmen were constantly underfoot on the campus. But let's get back to Howard our harassed friend.

The English program was just getting underway when he applied. He was a native speaker of English with a certificate qualifying him as a teacher of English as a Second Language. He had taught English for years in a language school in the city center. The first year was chaos for everyone with constant mistakes and changes in programs, teachers and teaching methods. He explained how they were struggling to get the course underway and the opportunities and challenges. It was too late to apply and get in on the current year, but I did apply for the following year and was accepted. They treated my master's degree like a doctorate. I already had a residence permit. The university was happy to have me. I was qualified for my work and humbly grateful to God for new opportunities. I had already worked for a Muslim school and had an introduction into the problems of state-private school tensions. I had worked in English language schools and knew the problems the city students faced. As a university teacher I was in a position where I could influence a system as well as individuals. The interplay between teachers, students and administrators, offered ample opportunities for the exchange of ideas and concepts; an opening to those influences, which I would define as Christian. Without building foreign financed institutions we could expose people to outside concepts and show them the wider world. It turned out to be an upturn in our work and we were accepted for what we were Western educators and at the same time sincere Christians. But I didn't continue teaching alone; Canadian volunteers applied and were accepted during the next three years. Hazel also joined in as the student counselor--super-mom to 400 students: a contact for those with problems and grievances. Three, two year volunteers, served. (All were retired teachers. Privately our local program was humorously titled by us as Geriatric Outreach, - GO!) Mary came as the last trickle of those efforts but she wasn't retirement age.

When Mary had gotten her own place, she had invited her former Turkish language helper (who was a student of Marshall's at the University) to share her apartment. It was a perfect location -- barely ten minutes walk from the University and minibus route -- and two minutes from the commuter train station. The next year, one of her students of the first year, asked if she could come to live there too. There were three bedrooms, so lots of space.

One of the volunteers, Roberta, after her first two years, went back to Toronto to study voice. When it was time for Mary's furlough, Roberta was contacted to see if she would come back and take Mary's place the year she was away. Roberta accepted and kept the house in order. She stayed over for more time. She became interested in working with the Gypsies. She has maintained contact with several of the students of those first two classes that she taught. She has made trips back for special events (weddings) and entertained several of them back in Canada.

Nancy, an American, taught at Marmara and served a number of years under our watch care.

Frank and Vera added the Middle East as another listing in their incredibly long service as volunteers around the earth in at least seven countries: Zaire, Kenya, Indomesia, Turkey, India, Bolivia and Brazil. Volunteers in their eighties are worth watching.

I, Marshall, was cast first in the role of phonetics teacher and I went through the English sounds and the strangeness of our open and closed vowel system. I knew the problems the students would have with: W, TH, R, unaccented A, and consonant clusters. We tackled these in a step-by-step, consistent way. Many new students thought that they spoke well. It was enough to be understood and communicate in the language level they had. So I had some resistance; always from those who were convinced that they already knew English, but through someone else's fluke in the placement test, had failed. The humble beginners made the best progress and with training many spoke without accents.

I wrote a small text with my phonetic conclusions and used it the rest of my time there. However, I also assumed the audio-visual duties after Christmas.

Many of our Turkish fellow teachers were women who had studied in the U.S. or England. They had returned to marry doctors, engineers or businessmen and to supplement their early career by working until they could start their families. These young westernized women were open to friendships. The foreign teachers were wives of Turks, Christian workers, or young adventurers expanding their horizons. There was a double standard for teachers. Turks got a national standard salary. Foreigners got another standard, high enough to attract them from their home country, if the chance to work in another culture was part of the fascination of teaching. The positions drew a real assortment of people --young and old.

If these expatriates complained that they could not live on that salary, they were offered positions in local high schools, where they could get paid at the end of the month. First year teachers, had sometimes arrived, after borrowing money for their fare and were devastated when they did not get paid month after month. The University would advance them some toward their salary, but couldn't pay them until the end of the calendar year, when their contracts kicked in. So "room and board" was provided. (We were never offered this option since it was obvious that we were already established with an apartment and all. It was three years later when we found out that we could have been having all of our meals in the university dining room!) At the end of the year, the university received the rest of their budgeted money. Directors of departments would do all they could to get this money and divide it up among the teachers so that they all have a portion until the new budget was approved. Moonlighting was encouraged.

If that still was not enough, there were almost daily calls to the University office, asking for teachers to tutor privately. When one of the local hospitals wanted a teacher to upgrade the staff's English, the Administration thought I was just the proper person. However, it meant giving up my lunch hour. The drive over took 20 minutes (chauffeured in a hospital vehicle) an hour for class and another 20 minutes to return. The pay was supposed to include lunch at the hospital cafeteria, but I never got in on that because there was no time, and several times I was late to class. A couple of times I took Hazel along to model and stimulate dialogue. So when I was given another job at that hour, I just sent her, and she had a great time the rest of the term. Over the dinner table they were much more relaxed and the learning opportunities continued. When they were well acquainted, she was able to help the dietitian understand some of the books that came in English related to her work, and a young pediatrician also had a couple of private sessions. When we were leaving to come to Canada, they gave her a farewell party with gifts to remember them by.

We earned about $500.00 a month per teacher and this money was used to pay local group expenses for all the personnel. We did not receive money directly from Canada but it was banked in our individual accounts at home and drawn on by check in times of need. Marshall first, and later Tom as treasurer drew money for direct payment of rents, transport or supplies if local salaries were insufficient to cover them. Unlike many fields the money did not have to be sent in U.S. funds: Canadian dollars would do, it was a big saving.

The hours were full and the days long. We had teachers meetings with updating studies each term and planning sessions as well. A chance off-hour was filled at school with grading papers or preparing for class. To be the best, the top of our teaching profession, was our goal as Christian witnesses. Many of our students thought we were. Our directors, however, always found areas that needed bettering.

Our students were formed into classes that reflected level and ability of the group. The advanced knew lots of English and were harder to keep happy. Beginners lagged at first, but the year's end could produce surprises.

The relation with students was a mix. Every class had teachers they liked and those they liked less, and some times less and less. Personal qualities and character counted for more and more as time passed and relations became closer. Mentoring became a possibility. It was our prayer that some would catch a glimpse of Jesus.

Wisdom calls aloud in the street, she raises her vioce...
Proverbs 1:20

You are talking ... foolish...
Shall we accept good from God,
and not trouble?
Job 2:10

26

WHO TOOK THE SULTAN'S HEAD?

"Mr. Thompson, please come to Ahmet bey's office immediately." I was in the first half-hour of a two-hour afternoon class. It was spring and they were in constant danger of going slack and losing concentration if they had time to dream instead of work. I tried to put off the summons.

"I'll come at the hour break." The messenger looked annoyed.

"No," he said, "NOW! It's urgent." I promised the class I would be back immediately and gave them something to do. I accompanied the messenger. I wondered if Hazel was ill.

The office was full of solemn people. A hefty, bald man proclaimed pompously (reading from an official looking letter) that I was being accused of having stolen and sold the head of Sultan Ahmed IV to the Metropolitan Museum in New York. I couldn't believe my ears. I asked Ahmet bey if someone in the office would be able to translate it. I more or less thought I understood the meaning. He translated, and sure enough that's what the man had read: that I had been accused of unearthing a sculptured head of Sultan Ahmed IV in the town of Ushak.

I had been cautioned over and over again not to take anything from an historic site, nor even buy anything that might have historic significance, since I could never take it back to North America. It was against the law.

I asked Ahmet bey if this could be attended to after class. He looked at me strangely and said the matter needed immediate attention. I was free to go with the police now. I turned and rushed back to my class with a thin little man following. I assigned them an English language video to watch. I then returned with my watchdog to the office where the official joined us. At street level it appeared that the men had no transportation. "Would you please flag a taxi, it would be quicker." I did and I paid.

Hazel met me at the door surprised that I was early from class, and forcing a calm in my voice that I did not feel, explained that the men were here to search our house. She invited them in with as much grace as she could muster and asked if she could offer them a glass of tea. The official, very stiffly and with exaggerated politeness informed her that it was necessary for her to be present during the search. She should go into the living room, unlock any cabinets and sit down.

She still hadn't understood as yet, what it was that was lost. He went through the buffet, shelf by shelf (allowing her to put the linens, vases, china, etc. back when he had finished.) I think he must have figured that if we were going to hide something, behind the linens would be a logical place. Then he started on the china closet. All of a sudden, Hazel gave a sharp little cry and ran for the kitchen. When she heard that spitting sound that a pot makes when it is boiling dry, she remembered the cauliflower that she had put on to cook before their arrival. Her mouse-like squeal startled us all. His lackey went running after her (so she couldn't go off and hide the head in another place, I suppose). He laughed when he saw the object of her concern and smiling accompanied her to the living room after she had removed the pot and added water.

Back in the living room, he found some photos from our first trip out to eastern Turkey. Almost every year we had gone visiting historic sites. We had accompanied friends, from the US or Canada, three or four times around the Seven Churches of the Revelation. So he asked her if she could identify the places, and the ones she could, she did. He wondered if we had visited the Metropolitan Museum in New York. Though we had passed through the New York airport many times, we had only spent the night in the city once, and that had been more than 30 years before! We had been arranging for shipping our things to Bolivia, so had never had time to visit that prestigious institution. When he took Hazel's stone collections and dumped them into one bowl her curiosity got the better of her. We had gone to a camp with the Turkish church where we attended on Sunday afternoons. That was on the Aegean Sea and she had collected a handful of shells, broken green glass worn by the movement of the tides and brightly colored marble chips. I say, brightly colored, but that's only if wet. So, in those early days when she first got her china closet, she had displayed them in a clear plain drinking glass of water, to have something to show off. Then, when we visited the Black Sea, she found some more. The Mediterranean yielded yet others, so there were three glasses of small sea mementos. When he began to paw through them she asked how big the sultan's head was. He assured her that it was life-sized. I expect that he was looking to see if there were any jewelry or small fragments with writing which would identify them as coming from some historic site.

Meanwhile, the second man was going from room to room inspecting the contents of each. The month before one of the workers had received a large shipment of literature that he had deposited in his apartment. Several of us had agreed to take six packets each because he hadn't enough space for all of it under his bed and tables. I had taken the goods begrudgingly. I don't believe in using literature that has to be hidden. We had adopted the policy of conforming to local custom by not doing those things which openly provoke local authorities and are considered mass produced Christian propaganda. There are groups who specialize in confrontation with the law in order to force recognition of their constitutional rights to religious freedom. These packets were in the storeroom and I was worried about their discovery.

I decided to open one of the packages and show the man their contents and explain that it belonged to a friend, whatever the cost. The little man took one look, turned up his nose and showed no further interest in my confession.

They wrote on a paper something for us to sign: to the effect that they had treated us with due respect, had not entered forcefully, taken anything away, nor subjected us to any violence. We could hardly read it. Our Turkish instruction had not included any "legalese" before, so we were reluctant to sign it, but had no choice. To my surprise this did not end the matter.

They took me by taxi (I paid) to the police station where he and a new young man also in civilian dress asked me many questions, trying to trip me into saying I had done it. They also made statements about my history in Turkey. This showed me that they had an intimate knowledge of my life there. My old post office box in Sisili, apartment numbers, banks etc. Someone took down all I said in the interview, and I had to sign that paper as well. During that part of the investigation, it came out that this was done in 1966 or 1967, at dates when we were in Canada. My passport could prove that, but these facts didn't seem to impress them.

It seems that five or six local Turkish men from Ushak had been hired to dig for a man named Marshall. Three men swore that they had dug up the Sultan's head and he had taken it away with him. They had seen pictures of me and swore I was the man. I imagine that the head was in the Museum, and they were just hoping to find something ELSE that I hadn't managed to smuggle out of the country yet. He ended the conversation with the threat,

"I know you took that, and sold it, and I'm going to get you for it!" spoken with gritted teeth and extremely hostile bitterness. I understood his indignation. The robbery of national treasures is a crime against a nation. My inadequate reply was that I had never taken any relic, I would never take any relic and they were not going to make me leave Turkey. But I knew they could if they would. They thought me over qualified for the job and salary I got. There had to be some hidden angle. It was after 9 p.m. when they released me, I took a minibus home to a worried wife and friends.

The next evening on Television there was a program done by the Department of Antiquities of the Turkish Government raising awareness of the many national treasures that lay in Museums in New York, London, Berlin, and other capitols of the world. They were making an all out effort to recover these artifacts in order to show them in their own museums. I suppose some of my teaching colleagues may have considered me suspect from that time forward, but a few who thought better, came to find out how it turned out. One American teacher at our University had been there long enough to remember a Dr. Marshall who was an archeologist, and figured that he was the man they were mistaking me for.

We were planning a trip to India during the winter break. We were apprehensive, wondering if we should cancel. Perhaps we would not be able to get back into the country. What if they wouldn't give us an entry visa on our return? We consulted a number of Turkish friends, and decided to write a letter --in Turkish-- saying that our bags had been searched as we left the country and were devoid of any Turkish artifacts. This we presented to the person who went through our things on departure, but since it was 8 PM Saturday evening when we were leaving, the head of the department was not on duty and if we had had to use it as a document, it probably would not have had any legal value. But yet again, keen suspicion and zeal had succumbed to bureaucratic indifference. We never heard anything more about it. We had a beautiful, exciting and blessed trip. I had promised to take my wife to India 35 years earlier, before we were married. We thought it was the Lord's calling. Promises kept are better late than never. Things do work together for good. Expectations are fulfilled for those who wait.

The Lord has many ways of proving our resistance to error; but it is, at times, costly. We are allowed to show our convictions by our actions. We suppose we know His will but sometimes it involves detours and a calling that is temporary to cause us to make certain plans and actions that in the end will be changed to something different and perhaps, for us, better. But these things cannot be easily discerned this side of eternity.

Since you ignored all my advice and would not accept my rebuke, I in turn will laugh at your disaster ... When calamity overtakes you like a storm.
Proverbes 1:25; 26a; 27a

27

M. JOHN

THE FAMILIES, GOVERNMENTS AND SOCIETY in the Middle East treat with great severity young people who leave their religion of birth and convert to any other faith. Many, even parents, will tolerate indifference to its teachings and practice in daily life, which leads eventually to the personal loss of traditional faith. Even sceptisism or contempt of it is usually endured. However, the discovery of a new, dynamic faith that replaces the status quo is unacceptable and strongly opposed.

Such a one was Mohammed John. That was his name, although he preferred the last name as his first. He was young, handsome and had become a Christian in Tehran, his native city in Iran, seven years before. He had moved in and we wondered if he would ever move out. Here is why.

My friend Howard, recently married and having guests at his house already, had a young Christian friend who was planning to marry in two weeks. He was boarding at the home of the girl he wanted to marry. All I had to do was keep the boy for two weeks: because as a Christian, it was a bad testimony to have them living in the same house before the wedding. It was February. I was busy at university with an increase of video responsibilities in that year's English classes. I was behind on grading and had a student helper to get through with all the written material. Hazel was working at the University as student counselor as well, so we were away from home all day. Howard promised me John would be out all day with a new job and wouldn't be eating with us. Since I am susceptible to attacks of guilt over how blessed and well off I am. I

131

felt that it wouldn't hurt to put up with a bit of inconvenience for the ease of the young man John, and of Howard.

After Howard's guests left, his wife developed severe back spasms and was in constant pain. The doctors prescribed complete bed rest and a regime of mild exercises. No stress was to be permitted. John could not move back there.

It was true; John was gone all-day and late into the evening selling plastic bags to stores and shops. I would finish my supper and be doing the homework papers when he would arrive, footsore and weary. He was also hungry because he was too busy to eat. If we had some leftovers he would appreciate it, he said. Hazel would stop her work to warm something up. He would sit where I worked at the dining room table and eat and tell me all of the witness opportunities, victories or woes of the day. He always told everything in intricate detail. He liked eye contact to maintain interest in his activities and would put his hand on my arm or cover the pile, if I tried to look at the papers I was to grade. He would talk on and on about all that had happened that day and in the past. I couldn't excuse myself and leave for he had the habit of following you around while he talked. It was good Turkish practice except that his home language was Persian (Farsi), so he had an accent and a limited vocabulary. It was a second language for both of us. It created pauses, word search and questions.

He was a bold fervent witness for Christ. He had written up his story in good Turkish with the help of a friend, and then had another friend translate it into English, so that you could know about his experiences and why he was in Turkey.

It all started in his late teens. Some Christians invited him to services at a nearby church. He was the youngest child in a large family of about ten children. He accepted Jesus with joy, and started trying to witness to his family as well. However, they were strict Muslims, and horrified that he had been "taken in" by those believers. They tried everything to get him to give it up. When he wouldn't, they sent him away to the war.

It was during the war with Iraq, and they called the "recruiters" to come and get him; take him into the armed forces and see that he would be killed. Then, his family would be exonerated, and not blamed that he had been proselytized. He went into the service, and was sent to the front with many other young men. (We could understand that --the streets of Istanbul were full of young Iranians whose families had sent them to Turkey to study so they <u>wouldn't</u> be killed in the war.) Sure enough, assigned to the most dangerous positions, as agreed by his family, he was gravely wounded almost the first time they engaged the enemy. They sent him to his hometown to a local hospital. The family was assured that he couldn't live. The father never came to see him, I'm not sure of the rest of his family, but somehow his church found out he was in the hospital. They called the church together and prayed, and then some of them went to the hospital and prayed. He was miraculously healed.

A civilian once more, the family was still ashamed of him. They had done business with companies in Turkey, and got in touch with some of their contacts, and sent him to them. Upon arrival there, he looked up a church and somewhere along the way, found Howard.

After the first week of his living in our home we learned that the wedding had been postponed two weeks. He was sure we would understand. We knew we were stuck.

We should explain that the local Christian council met regularly, had seminars and presented papers on the work. The Muslim counter to conversion among their youth was to abandon the guilty one and withdraw all support and guidance. Since families arrange for the marriage and set them up in their first business experience, this left the boy out in the cold without a coat. We had agreed to provide a Christian family backing or home, advice and help under proper conditions. Many of us had the opportunity of housing and guiding young men. He was neither the first nor the last.

John was faithful in his Christian witness. He talked about it to the people he sold to. He sometimes got hostile answers, but he ignored them. He witnessed to the neighborhood kids and the guys on the team at Fener Bahche. He would come home and tell us about it every day. We had prayer together every night before retiring.

Here was a young man full of good intentions and he even gave away or sold bibles to some of his contacts. He was not shy in talking about Jesus. We realized again how difficult it is for young unsponsored men to get ahead. The social and economic system is stacked against them and their lack of experience.

John had two priorities besides marrying Selma. 1. He wanted to get a job that would support them. And 2. He wanted to get a contract to play soccer. He said he had been a star professional player back home, and enjoyed the limelight, prestige, and income associated with them.

This job selling plastic bags was great; every business needed them and every one was willing to take them; they just couldn't pay for them till the end of the month. This meant that his 'cash flow' was not regular. His father had made plastic bags back in Iran. He thought if only he could get hold of a plastic-bag-making machine, he could go into the business for himself! He found a bargain on one. Couldn't we just help him out? Pressure began to build up for us to contribute toward this cause. Of course, once he got the machine, there would be a need for a place to install it; materials to make the bags from; etc., etc., etc.. He would take no advice. Many stores forgot their debts to him. He ran out of cash and credit. He couldn't buy any more bags to sell. People don't learn if you always bail them out of their troubles. I was unable and unwilling to intervene or invest. He got the same answers elsewhere. None of the families were financially able to help. The amount needed was high. His heedless nature and irresponsibility were well known.

When it came to light that we would not be able to help him get set up in business, depression set in. He postponed the wedding yet again. He would come in at night and tell me his troubles, but I had arranged to do papers at other times and places. I was careful not to get behind again. I actually feel this lessened his time spent in confidences. But now he did not want to report on his efforts to find a job.

Spring came and he had lost his product and job and refused to seek another. The business world was hard to crack and didn't pay enough for marriage anyway. He knew where the big money was: in sports. Football practice was going on all over the city for soccer, which they call *futbol*. It is the national sport. John had played on a professional team back in Iran as a goaltender. He was good so the Fener Bahche team let him practice with them. He came home with the news, he would soon be in big money. He was sure that Fener Bahche was going to hire him. He would come home bruised and tender with scrapes on shins and knees. He bragged about them not getting a goal when he was goalie.

Hazel would feed him. I would rub him down with Ben-gay or rubbing alcohol and paint his scratches. When the contracting time came and went, and the contract hadn't materialized, depression became deeper. We think he was at home most of the day.

Several times during his stay with us he called home, or wrote to say when he would be in so they could call him at our house. Then he would receive a call from his sister. He would beg her to let him talk to his father, but his father would yell from the background that he would talk to him when he returned to the true faith--meaning Islam. He would always feel very low at those times.

He didn't go out to look for a job any more. Someone lent him a videotape about the life of Pele, of Brazil. The most famous soccer player in the world. It sounded to us like he was doing nothing but sitting there watching those films all day long. Though he hadn't gotten the job, he lived in the dream world of "Pro-futbol". His friend demanded money for the tape he had appropriated so I bought it to keep him out of trouble. At this point I told him I had not let my son live like the son of a rich man; and I wasn't going to let him continue living like one either. I gave him a letter with St. Paul's advice in 2 Thessalonians 3:10, "If any would not work, neither should he eat." We were preparing to leave the country, and I told him that he needed to make arrangements to get another place to live, as he would have to leave the house in two weeks. We spoke to several people, but none of them could take him. Howard finally found an Armenian Senior Citizens home where he could get a room until something else opened up. He dragged his feet till the last day.

He started packing, but left on the deadline day without finishing up. So when I came from work that day, I went into the room, picked up the rest of his things, and put them in a duffel bag that we were lending him to pack into. I also reclaimed the alarm clock, the Pele video, towels, and other things that he had appropriated while living at our house. I set the bag just inside the apartment door for John's arrival. He came late, but we prayed and he left in tears.

When John arrived at the Old Folks Home, he made himself useful, and everyone was immediately enchanted. He entertained them all, helped them haul the ones who needed it into and out of bed, and helped serve in the kitchen. They offered him a job and he stayed there several months. I relented and gave him the Pele football video and several others to show the people he was entertaining and evangelizing. He visited to tell us the good news.

After he left, some neighbors asked where John was. We said that he had moved out. "What about the T-shirts?" the man asked. "What T-shirts?" we asked. Seems that when he missed the job with Fener Bahce, he started a local team of kids acting as coach. Selma came over to help him. It was one of his forms of Christian witness. He made a deal with a businessman nearby to print up a big order of T-shirts with a team logo. Each team member was to pay for his own shirt, and it would be enough to buy the whole order. He did not ask if we would help buy the sport shirts: did not even mention that he had organized the team. There must have been about a dozen of the boys in the group. He couldn't get enough kids to pay for their shirts and the businesses in the neighborhood did not contribute either. Those who paid never saw their shirts. We were very sad; we didn't know who they were or how to help.

In November while we were back in Canada, we had news that Selma was baptized the 17th of November and they were married the 18th. Our Asian Side Church had rented a restaurant for Sunday morning service. So we met them there. He insisted we come visit his house. He had a job. He had acquired a computer for games and she was attending university. He still witnessed for Christ. Our friendship continued.

We all have friends who stretch us and who are as imperfect as we are. In Christ, differences can be overcome and much can be learned from those whose life style bothers us.

*You shall teach these words to your children
and talk to them as you sit in your home
and when you walk along the road, when
you lie down and when you get up.*

Deuteronomy 6:7

For wisdom will enter your heart, and knowledge will be pleasant to your soul, Discretion will protect you and understanding will guard you.
Proverbs 2:10,11

28

MORE OF U.

AT MARMARA UNIVERSITY THINGS WERE coming along. Chaos decreased. Order increased. Classes were gaining in knowledge and the teachers growing confident by experience. Despair had changed to hope and enthusiasm.

We had a doctor of Audio-visual learning and bought tapes at his suggestion. However, he did not like the climate, which caused allergies in his daughter. His wife was Turkish but they had met in California and married. Returning to her home country some years later, when they planned to settle, he found many reasons for not staying. I was using simple dramas and dialogue situations in class and found myself being pushed toward greater involvement in the Audio-visual department. It was finally dropped in my lap when our experts spent the winter break in the States, and just never came back. I had help: an American lady married to a Turk, Victoria, helped organize the programmed use of film. We developed a useful curriculum. She even devised a way of scoring the days language performance. I made some changes and passed it to the sub-director, Marvin. The general director loved it with the adaptations made by the sub, but gave me the credit for bringing it forward. We got that straightened out eventually to my video lady's satisfaction. She was able to participate in an international forum on teaching English as a Second Language. By that time our director had accepted an offer in Japan and our sub was now director and participated in the forum in San Antonio, Texas. I think Victoria had a real sense of achievement. I had a sense of relief.

By this time I had become aware of the tremendous amount of gossip, politics and rivalry that exists among a school's personnel. Money and prestige are tied up in the race to get ahead. I had age on my side, but if I had been director I would have put Victoria as our department head, even if lots of people couldn't get along with her. She did a lot of the inspired written work sheets for use with each audiovisual tape. We got along well personally, although she was a complainer. When our general director left for a more profitable job, my Christian friend Marvin became general director and the school continued to improve. Other local universities came to study our language curricula and programs.

There were two major traumas every year: the start and the finish. Testing the new lot was the major fall event. Some who knew some English would hand in a blank paper thinking that it would be an easy ride starting from the beginning. They didn't count on getting bored and taking early advantage of the maximum absentee limits. This usually led to: missing some key unit which they hadn't studied or the danger of losing the whole year because of a late winter or spring illness or death in the family somewhere outside the city, necessitating a trip which would rob them of several days. It could also mean being a 'prisoner of the spring'. It was typical of the young to relax in the spring and have class outings. Those who had hoarded their limit of absences could indulge themselves after a hard fall and winters work, with a fair knowledge of the language. Those who had wasted theirs in early indulgence were sweating the exams and could not miss a single class day. Some had only a day or two left of permitted absence before expulsion. Enforcement was quite strict. These were the prisoners of the spring. If they were going to relax, they had to sleep in class. This the teachers, who were prisoners of their jobs, did not permit.

The people who thought they were knowledgeable in English were often the hardest to teach. They failed the placement test and had to take a year of something they thought they understood. They were indignant. There had to be a mistake. Someone did them in. They were sure they knew English. But they were not passed into English classes in business, medicine, or education. Some became our butterflies enjoying parties and maximum cuts of classes. I tried to make them keep journals in English. When you have to express your inner thoughts and important activities in another language you soon understand your limitations. We did interviews and investigative reporting starting with myself as the first subject and then bringing in special personalities in the spring.

Some students blossomed. others faded. We started weekly lectures on many subjects at the end of winter. Each professor took a two-hour lecture. Marshall spoke of the history of technology and conquests after the Roman empires: East and West. Each conqueror in turn had a religion or worldview, a dominant language, a capitol, and a specialized technology. Each ruled a large section of our present world. These were successively, the expansions of Islam, Catholicism, Orthodoxy, and Protestantism. All the lectures were well attended. Next year they all hoped to be in their specialty faculty attending lectures regularly. But roll was often not taken and some skipped classes. The student majority progressed, but there was ample evidence of individual failure and conflict.

There was a day of accounting near the end of the term. Those who did not have a total of 600 complete class hours (out of a possible 900) were not even admitted to the final exam; which represented one half of their final grade. There was always a great uproar when someone discovered that he/she couldn't take the final exam. Administration personnel were breaking their heads to find a solution so the students would spend as much time in class as possible. It was decided that they needed a student counselor.

The next year they got one. Hazel Thompson became "mother of four hundred".

The Director introduced her to each class in turn, and stated that they could take all their problems to her. In reality, her job description was to keep accurate records of the attendance, so that when a person came within 50 hours of losing the exam, they would be asked to talk to her. She would tell them how many hours there were left before they would lose the opportunity to take the final. Then she would explain that they were in danger of losing the whole year's work. She tried to find the reason for the absences, and if there was some way to help them.

She really had very little sympathy for those who were just playing off. But for a number of students, she was able to be an advocate for special treatment. One girl had surgery, and though she was not able to continue that year --she was admitted to the classes the next year without having to repeat the tests and all. One young man lost his father, and had to stop to go to work and support his family. She sought to help him find a job at other hours, so he could continue to be in class.

For a blind boy, she helped to secure a typewriter and table for his dorm room, so that he could do his homework (no, NO tables, desks, typewriters, wardrobes, or book cases, were usually permitted in the crowded dorms).

When Ataturk began his reforms in an effort to bring Turkey into the modern age, he outlawed the "*chadir*" (that coverall black robe worn by devout Muslim women), the "*shalvar*" (baggy pants, for both men and women) and the *fez* (for men). He really tried to get them to imitate western styles. Many women embraced this change wholeheartedly, and started looking to Paris for their mode of dressing. Other devout women in the cosmopolitan city of Istanbul had adapted to large headscarves with a raincoat, and sensible shoes. The styles of designs, colors, and ways of tying these scarves (so that not a strand of hair showed) changed from year to year, but they were still "conforming" to Islamic rules for dress.

With Ayatollah Khomeni's ascension to power in Iran, next door, Turkey was flooded with propaganda. It said that no decent woman would show her arms, shoulders or hair. Nobody objected to long sleeves when cool weather came, but wearing a headscarf was considered a veil, and those who wore them were often forced out of class by peer pressure. One Turkish teacher was seeing her class split over the issue, and determined to stand with the modern girls and throw the girl out. The girl came to me (Hazel) with a note from her mother, who asked to interview the director of the English Language program. The mother would mobilize public protests if we denied her appeal. I warned the director of her intent, and he said, "As long as she does her studies, I couldn't care less what she wears." He also knew the teacher he was dealing with, so withdrew the student from that class, and put her in one where there were a number of the "covered" girls already, and there was no objection to her manner of dress. I was very appreciative that he had made the decision, and I didn't have to. The larger University of Istanbul had been having strikes and protests, fighting over the issue, for a month. The media were having a ball showing mobs of protesting students, alumni, and mothers: in shoving and shouting matches with the police before the University gates. His decision pulled the teeth of violence for Marmara, though for a week we did have very tight security and wondered daily if we would get through the day safely. Our university "mother" handled protests on a personal level.

Marshall was asked to replace some of the teachers in special oral retrials where a person was on the border of failure and a year's loss. Some times the teacher would come with the request saying: "She wears a scarf, I'm not sure I can be impartial. You sit in for me." In most of these cases, the failure was evident in the language, not the scarf.

Ramazan was another particularly hard trial. Almost all the students would participate by abstaining from food by day and having a banquet meal after sunset and waking to a pre-dawn breakfast. It was a macho thing to do and boys could brag of their keeping up with custom and studies. Except they didn't. Grades dropped because those who lived at home had to keep the custom and the girls had to cook with mother. Those in dorms had friends who would invite them home for the special foods served at that time. Girls would also invite others and end up in the kitchen preparing and sampling everything. With less sleep by night and gorging they became more torpid by day, less alert. Grades sagged significantly. The study time and grades developed a permanent sag that corresponded with the 28 or 29 day lunar fast. Some of the teachers participated as well and tempers became shorter. The same phenomenon is noticed in industrial production.

Marshall sometimes participated for the first three days just to know how they were feeling. He found that it created sympathy toward his students rather than irritation, but that tempers were definitely shorter because of the experience. Fatigue was the end result, which did not disappear with the end of the fast. Depression followed fatigue; dropouts increased. It was hard to overcome the effects. If Ramazan came in the spring, the year ended in a down. In winter the effects were less severe as the nights are longer. In summer the days are long and the heat increases the fatigue. Fights increase police activity. Hospitals experience higher activity with less efficiency.

Faithful Muslims declare that the fast promotes health and togetherness in families. We were not in a position to dispute that statement, but it was death on education and amiability at school. We, like them, justify our customs and family practices as good and profitable. Yet all cannot be of equal value. How can we be impartial about things our culture approves? I, as a western Christian, can only hope that my attitudes, practices and life style demonstrated qualities worthy of imitation.

Jesus' formula for testing worth was found in His words: "by their fruits you will know them." Yet, even here, we have difficulty testing our fruit. Arguments about results and value can be endless. Judging is difficult business. God is the final judge, which is the safest place to leave the matter.

Yes, establish the work of our hands.
Psalm 90:17

29

ALL ABOUT CHURCH

ALTHOUGH THE COUNTRY OF TURKEY is 98% Muslim the cities are full of churches. Some still function as churches to pitifully reduced congregations; others have been converted into museums, music concert halls, warehouses, tourist sites or mosques. The earliest church, third century Hagia Irene, is a concert hall with marvelous acoustics. The enormous sixth century Hagia Sophia, the size of a football field, was finished by the Emperor Justinian and is a museum. Many are still beautiful though neglected, unless they earn their way like the first tourist attractions mentioned. Both Orthodox and Catholic churches show basically the same works in paintings or statuary: The virgin and the infant Jesus. Where a mother and child exist there must be a father, therefore, a Muslim reasons Christians must believe the Holy Trinity is a Family; that God took a wife to whom many Christians pray. Pluralities of God are an abomination to the monotheistic Muslim. But all these ancient and modern churches agree by their internal decorations. Mary appears as important as Jesus. The evidence is overwhelming.

Only the Protestant churches present a different appearance and reality. The Word, both living and written, rules above all. It is written on the walls and on posters in their churches. Jesus is God's word of salvation and truth for all nations, religions and individuals. God was made flesh and word for our example. We are His body and living letters to be read by all and to serve as He wills.

We went to church every Sunday, sometimes -- two or three times – and after we moved to the Asian side, we could always come home to our house church at night. You would call our Sundays strenuous. From Europe it was half an hour, but from Asia it was two hours by bus, ferry and subway (Tünel) or shared taxi to the Dutch Chapel, named for the Consulate property on which it had been built centuries ago. The American Board missionaries met for worship in homes for 17 years before they moved into the Dutch Chapel. The body of believers called itself the Union Church of Istanbul. The "rent" is "Prayer for the reigning Dutch Monarch". All the church services are in English. After our fifth year, there were two services and we favored the early one. The sanctuary would hold 100 comfortably, and 130 uncomfortably! Before the congregation grew to the point that we needed two services, the children went downstairs after the "children's" story for Sunday School. The trouble was that they hated to ask anyone to teach it full time, because there was only that ONE service of worship a week. So one person coordinated and asked a different teacher to teach one month at a time. When we first got really crowded, we just asked the parents to bring the children straight into the Sunday School room and drop them off and had a worship service just for them. Then God sent a teacher whose call was teaching children.

Tourist buses often made the early service their first stop for those who wanted to visit a church there. Then they would return to the hotel to pick up the others who had slept in.

We were in a real period of growth, though, and the children's extra 30 seats quickly filled up again. So we discussed and then eventually started two services. This meant that those who were teachers did not have to sacrifice their worship time, but could come to the early service, and then teach afterward.

Our years in Bolivia, had been so busy with other pursuits that we had little time for choral music. Our first Sunday in the Dutch Chapel, Marshall, when visitors were recognized, stated a desire to sing in the choir. So we were approached afterwards by Bill, the choir director. who invited us to rehearsal on Wednesday night at eight. That started an activity that lasted ten years. There was only room for about a dozen to sit in the choir loft over the entrance facing the pulpit. When we had an occasional visitor who would sing with us, they sometimes had to sit on the stairs, just joining us on the upper level, when we stood to sing. During those ten years, Marshall tried to get a fan installed against the unbearable heat of summer, but never managed it.

Besides the regular Sunday morning worship service, Bill prepared and presented a baroque concert in early December with full choir and orchestra. With 35 in the choir and 15 in the orchestra, we had to perform in other places to have room for the audience. Sometimes we performed in a church: the Catholic one down the hill, the Italian one along Istiklal Boulevard, the Armenian one across the Bosphorus, or the German Luthern one nearby. Several times it was the ballroom of the British Consulate, and once at the German consulate. These usually seated two to three hundred people; expatriate Christians and their invited friends. You can imagine how excited we were when we were invited to present the <u>Messiah</u> in a University. The auditorium would accommodate 600. It was packed, and though we sang in English, the printed program gave a Turkish translation.

It took so long to get home to Asia from church that we made a practice of eating at a small cafeteria right on the main street near the Dutch Chapel. Many of the other worshipers joined us there, because they also had come a long way. It was a great time of fellowship. Then, in the afternoon, we joined a Turkish-speaking group in worship. They worshipped in the basement of that same Catholic church down Istiklal. When they needed the meeting place for another activity on Sunday afternoon, we moved down Istiklal to an Armenian Catholic Church.

At the beginning we bought a hymnal so we could learn the hymns. People suggested that we wait to buy a Bible because the language was so antiquated and only people older than us used that kind of language any more. We still bought one; and did regular readings with friends, national or foreign, who knew the language well. We had to buy an old, old dictionary in order to find out what some words they used meant.

Two Protestant groups were translating the New Testament, actually two very different translations — but they didn't come out until about 8 years later. Many of the words had been changed. We had to buy a new dictionary to understand the new words that were being used in the daily newspaper. And, there were new words being added to the language daily.

The Koreans have become a large part of God's gospel outreach in Turkey. They are well received because Turks were allies of the South Koreans and fought heroically in the Korean War. Let me tell you how their first church group started at the Dutch Chapel. The Koreans started as a trickle into the Dutch Chapel with one entrepreneur with his wife and two young boys. They had been in Germany for a couple of years, but moved to Turkey, and began to attend the church. She had a beautiful voice and sang solos as well as both of them helping in the choir.

The Korean Trade Center also had a young couple, the wife having been a worker in another middle eastern country. She joined a few of us in an international Bible study group. When their term was up, they were followed by another, and another. The third couple had a four-year-old girl, Minki, and a 13-month-old toddler. Minki came to Sunday School, although she knew no English, while the baby boy stayed with Mother. She attended with the first families two boys, who had by now picked up some Turkish and English, and could translate for her. Minki was the darling of the whole group (which included besides the dominant English; Greek, French, and Spanish speakers).

Not many Koreans came to church, but in the evening, the whole colony would meet at the trade center for a potluck meal. The Korean Trade Center was five stories up in a building overlooking Taksim Square: and was ancient and quaint. The elevator took forever to get up and down and it's doors were wrought iron.

One lovely August evening about 5 o'clock, Minki's little brother escaped unnoticed to the balcony, climbed over the banister, and fell to the pavement below. Everyone went scurrying out, some on the elevator, and others racing down the narrow stone staircase. The Mother snatched up her son, and her husband started the car and off they went to the hospital. And then another—and then another. "There is no Pediatrician on duty..." "We have no facilities for treating children..." "There are no beds open..." "There is no Doctor on call..." One after another they were turned away from eight hospitals. Finally, the American Hospital took them in, although they had the same problems as the other national hospitals, but at 4 in the morning, the baby died in his mother's arms. Our pastor was away, but another one in the congregation had been left in charge, and we were called to stand by this family in their need. A number of the members at the Dutch Chapel came to the small Protestant chapel in the cemetery.

Since we had to come after classes, we were a little late, and ran into a Korean man who had come all the way from Ankara, and didn't know where he should go. We found it together. The tiny cemetery chapel was packed with the choir on one side, and the entire Korean community on the other side. The distraught mother clung to the casket, and did not want to leave, but we and the Korean friends did what we could to comfort her. They told us that, though the father was not able to join his wife for the trip, she left the next day for some time with her family back in Korea.

We were in for a shock the next Sunday: at that time we had three families who were attending. That Sunday, there were eleven of fourteen families. Many of the wives did not even speak either English or Turkish. But they all trooped in with all their kids. There were 27 in all. Up to then the Korean children had been mixed with the others, but we knew that we would have to draft that first lady to teach all those children. They had a whole table to themselves.

And they came faithfully. Up until then we had had the use of the Dutch Chapel only on Sunday, but they asked if they could use it on Saturday morning to have a Bible class, and also help the children learn Turkish, and Korean—so they wouldn't lose home language. For some months then we didn't have the crowds, because they were teaching the children on Saturday. Then they started having services in someone's home. One young Korean man, the first who came to share his faith at a university, began to serve as their pastor. It was about that time that we left for furlough. When we returned, we heard that they were back meeting at the chapel. They had sent back to Korea for a Pastor, and were having their Sunday meetings in the Chapel once more. By then we were involved in another church group, but were invited especially by a Korean friend to come to visit them in afternoon worship. We went and found a congregation of about 80 persons. We were so impressed with their pastor. He preached the same sermon in Korean, Turkish, and English that afternoon. Idea by idea, he spoke to his compatriots, to us who spoke English, and to those local visitors who spoke Turkish! We were introduced as honored guests, who had been there at the funeral— and had stood by the family who lost their baby boy. By then Minki was about 10 years, old, and the little brother she lost had been replaced with another the very next year after she lost him. They tell me that they never told her that her baby brother died. It was not their custom, they said. But they traced the beginnings of their church to that time of our congregation standing by the family in their time of loss.

When we returned from our home time, Tom and Gladys, had started meeting for a meal on Sunday evening with Howard and Claudia. After the meal they would have an informal service in English. They asked if we would like to join them, and little by little, others wondered if they might come, too. As numbers increased a meal became too much, so we served tea, coffee, and finger food as a fellowship time after the service.

None of these people were our university students, however. There was a mix of foreigners, students from elsewhere, and local people from near by. The neighbors watched us through the open windows. They found it strange that we sat to pray and sing and stood to eat after the meditation. We always sang one verse of our songs in Turkish so the outsiders would know of whom we were singing. One weekend the family had to travel and they changed the meeting to our house. The next week after their return an astonishing number of neighbors inquired worriedly why the meeting had been canceled and the apartment dark on Sunday night.

Months after that, we moved the meetings to our house which had a large living-dining room which could accommodate more people. The regulars agreed not to come if they had an invitation from a national for talks or excursions where witnessing could take place. A Friday meeting was largely for prayer and exchange of information about the work. In my last year of teaching we agreed to change and hold a special Friday worship service for a secretive group of Americans who had not fellowshipped with other Christian workers. They became conscious of this as a flaw, even a sin. They wished to open their ranks for companionship. It was a kind of repentance and there was a very definitely good effect from this action. We eventually moved the meeting to Sunday night and then started seeking an external place. We had no more room to grow.

At the end of my last year of teaching at Marmara University I moved household furnishings and packed boxes into a house we helped rent, to hold our things, until we could return. Our friends Jim and Karen also put their furniture there until their home assignment was finished. There was one tiny room near the main door where a single worker lived. It was rent-free if he/she would act as janitor and guardian of our collective goods. We didn't lose a thing.

When the congregation moved to our house we served tea afterward with sweet cookies and salty crackers. When the leak occurred at the Chernoble atomic plant in the Ukraine, the tea cultivating areas in Turkey were contaminated. Supplies of uncontaminated tea were soon sold out, because Turks drink a lot of tea. Marshall and I drink it sparingly, but usually bought in great quantities for our economy's sake, so we had lots on hand, and we also had a number of herbal teas. We told people that our tea was pre-Chernoble when we invited them, and perhaps some came just for the tea after that. We also bought fruit crystals and served them hot, too.

We took turns bringing the message at first, but when the group began to grow, it was only the men who spoke. Now before you get excited and protest—we really prayed about it when we began to have some Turkish friends join us. The idea was to share the Gospel, and we realized that some Turkish men would never hear the words if they came from a woman. In a Bible study it was different, but if it was a prepared message, we decided to follow the local pattern.

Tom served as treasurer during this period. His visa came from his official retirement papers from Edmonton University where he had worked with the audio-visual equipment. All Turks found it logical that he should leave the land of igloos and wish to retire in Turkey. As long as his spending passed a designated sum he would be permitted to stay. He and Gladys had a hospitality house where young people could rest, study, talk out problems and eat when they felt the need. Tom never forgot a face or a name. Many friends were won by their open house policy.

I did not realize that I would not have a job at the university on my return from home assignment. The University had been changed, restructured, and caught in a budget pinch. The church was renting a night club (the revelers were through with it before Sunday School time) and becoming more public. We could not find housing in the former community. We would find a new task and a new arena of witness. Our partners had moved to another community near by. Everything had changed. God does not allow His workers to become too comfortable; there are always new challenges. He made all things new, with problems to solve, again and again. You can be happy in these circumstances, if you are relaxed and prayerful, leaning on the Lord.

Marshall & Hazel Thompson

Whatever happens, conduct yourselves in a manner worthy of the Gospel of Christ.
Philippians 1:27P

30

FASHION BY DESIGN

CLOTHES ARE MORE THAN SIMPLE protection against the elements. They are a statement of the social and economic status of the wearers. They also can indicate local areas of origin or work and special rank, or marital status of the person. Uniforms indicate specialty and service. These signs are read automatically by members of a culture. We use fashion to show or hide what we desire others to see or not to see. Fashion is always by design.

There are some other signs: in Turkey, "covering" was important to the devout Muslim woman. In Istanbul--the stylish woman who was also devout (or whose father or husband was and demanded it) -- wore a scarf that showed nothing of her hair. She wore dresses that didn't show her arms -- even in the terrible heat of summer. She wore sensible shoes. If her dress had short sleeves, she wore a light raincoat on top of it. At home, she didn't have to do this, but she usually had her scarf around her neck. Then, if someone came to visit, she put it on properly on the way to the door. If it was another lady or a member of the family she could relax and put it back down around her neck, ready for the next such emergency.

The first sixteen-month period we spent in the Middle East I only saw four women dressed in that long, black, head-to-toe covering (that is worn in Iran, Saudi Arabia and some other Middle Eastern countries), called the *chadir* in Turkey.

During the time Ayatola Khomeni was in power in Iran, Turkey was flooded with propaganda, calling Muslim women to a "return to decency"--which meant, "being covered".

In my youth, I remembered pictures of the "Babushka", the little old Russian grandmother in her colorful scarf, who I somehow presumed was "orthodox" Christian. In South America, I was accustomed to seeing the Catholic women wearing their scarves, especially in church. So when I heard of one of our Christian friends, who had forbidden his wife to wear a scarf, I was shocked! It was winter, and a very damp and chilling one --pneumonia weather-- so I asked him why? Seems he was afraid that she would be taken for a Muslim! How else could you tell who is a Christian? I suggested that she pull her shawl (she had a nice warm, wooly one) up over her head.

I don't know if he vetoed that or not.

When Ataturk tried to bring Turkey into the modern world, he outlawed wearing the turban, the fez, the *chadir*, the *shalvar* (baggy pants), and many other items and customs that he felt were deterring progress in his country. If you saw someone in the city dressed in a *shalvar*, you knew they were visiting from the country. Traveling in the countryside, you frequently saw people wearing them, or women with the *chadir*. What village policeman is going to enforce the law in those things, when it's his grandmother wearing them?

There are many in Turkey today who follow the fashions of Paris, or Italy, or their own fashion designers who are equally talented. Most wear the secular current clothes accepted in business or at social occasions everywhere. The religious, too, are today enjoying modern dress. The devout rich may purchase each year a new wardrobe full of raincoats that are "decent", but cut a different way and scarves with different designs, and are tied a different way, and shoes that have a different heel, or straps, or colors. And the devout working girl will follow those styles in less expensive materials. They are the signs of belonging to a moral majority.

In our visits to North American churches we were able to give real examples of how the people dressed and why they preferred certain styles. This involved carrying a number of typical costumes with us and giving a fashion show. We discovered that some Muslim students who came at the invitation of their Christian friends were as happy with our displays and explanations as were the membership. This involved the use of local models, both young and old of both sexes. We had excitement as the differences between rural and city clothes were explained and illustrated.

Hazel first called up the three ladies and one man. Giggles, oohs and ahs accompany the presentation. She starts her fashion show with a brightly striped satin outfit that consists of quite straight trousers with a draw-string, and a long sleeved jacket that does not quite meet in front.

But I'll let her tell it! The outfit has a sash, and I had them put it right over their blouse. There was a filmy scarf that went right across the top of a little pillbox hat and tied under the chin. I explained this was worn in the harem in olden times, but that today you would never see anyone dressed that way on the street unless they were on their way to a folkloric presentation. Some girls, who served the tea in a hotel, might also be dressed this way.

The next girl would wear a one-piece outfit made of a diaphanous material called *shile beize*, like the fine cotton called canvas, formally used under wallpaper in North America. It is beautifully embroidered and many tropical countries make blouses and caftan's from it. Down the outside of each leg, was painted an intricate Turkish design. It is shirred with elastic thread at the top, waist and ankles and is held up by spaghetti straps. I bought one pair for each of my girls to use as summer pajamas.

Every young tourist I ever saw making the rounds of the gift shops, said, "Isn't that cute!" and usually added, "And just what I need in this heat." They are really not very expensive. They come in a great variety of beautiful pastel colors and can be washed out and dried overnight, and put on again in the morning. So, she gets one or even two and wears them all the rest of her trip. For my model, I bought black because you couldn't see through it.

However, they are so revealing that no decent Turkish gentleman will even look at her straight. He can probably be heard muttering under his breath in passing, "These INDECENT, IMMORAL, CHRISTIAN WOMEN!" Both of the just described outfits are meant only for wearing inside the harem. The women who wore them—wives and concubines--belonged to the Sultan, and no man but he would ever see them that way. When they were allowed a ride in one of their carriages down the city streets, or boats on the Bosphorus, they had to be fully covered and veiled.

So when a young tourist buys one and wears it on the street, she's confirming the TV image of a loose and immoral person.

"Imagine," they think, "Wearing harem clothes in public, day or night on their tours."

On the other hand, the cleaning lady who came very stylishly dressed to help me clean house once a week, disappeared into the bathroom, and came out looking like something out of history. She would have on the *shalvar*. These were usually made of a really pretty calico print in an opaque cotton cloth. If you were to make a floor length skirt of three or four yards of cloth, cut an arc across the bottom, and sew it, then gather the outside around the ankles, you too could have a *shalvar*. When she stepped out onto the windowsill of my high-rise apartment building to wash my windows, NO ONE would EVER accuse HER of being indecent or immoral—even though she was a Christian! My model could be any size, and I always chose a model that was wearing a long sleeved blouse.

I had a black and red striped length of material a yard wide and twice that long, that the tea pickers on the Black Seacoast wore. It was pinned under the chin (or maybe even the nose) reached down to the waist in front and back and showed no hair. She started her walk-around with that on as I stated, "That is what she would wear harvesting in the field. In the house she would have a white *shile beize* scarf with an elaborate beaded edge that she had crocheted herself."

In the city, it would usually be a fine silk smaller one 27 "to 30" square. I would exchange one of those on the lady, and found that some husbands hadn't even recognized their own wives when they were dressed up that way. Dress makes a difference.

Most of our church models took to it nicely, while others were embarrassed. At an association rally one man accidentally loosed the waist string on the baggy *shalvar* and found himself trying to walk with them round his feet. The audience reacted with hysterical laughter, fortunately he had his pants on under them. Everyone had fun while learning the basic attitudes of the people of the Middle-East. They are really concerned for the outward look of the community while the Westerner is concerned with freedom to display.

We found village clothes sensible, loose fitting, comfortable for work or leisure. The pronounced low crotch on the village men's *shalvar* seems funny at first but they are comfortable in every position. My neighbor would point out how our tight, form fitting clothes were difficult to manage for sitting cross-legged on the couch or floor. Our Western clothes they counted as restrictive and self-consciously seductive in design. Only city people would wear such clothes, they say. Arranged marriages rather than seduction is the key to keeping dress plain and simple. You don't try to attract men, your parents chose you one and make the arrangements.

While living in a rural village during our last years in Turkey we made friends with the *Imam*, religious authority, in our village. I saw how concerned he was with the outward trappings of morality expressed in village life. Yet he despaired of the inward lack of the same morality. Jesus spoke of cleaning the exterior and the interior of the cup. Muslims are concerned about the clean outside of the cup but they don't know how to clean the inside. The *Imam* wished me to become a Muslim (one surrendered). I prayed for him to be a believer and follower of *Isa Mesih* (Jesus the anointed): both discovered something of God in our cordiality.

A neighbor had named his son for Jesus; *Isa* is his name. Since Catholic societies frequently name boys for Jesus, I was not surprised. He was a very handsome man, masculine and attractive in the village clothes. They had gotten for him a wife as beautiful and feminine in her village dress as any well-matched couple could be in any fashion. Their dress was simple, modest and beautiful; by contrast ours are fastidious, yet revealing and often uncomfortable.

I recognized in their naming of the son the same search for purity, integrity and high morals that we wish for those we love. We seek those who model that kind of life. We name our children after them. Jesus has that kind of life, for the internal and external cleansing of our life and offers it to the seeker. But he offers it on his terms, not on ours. He would be your new fashion. He wants your all, in obedience, now. It is basically all you have to offer.

My heart says of you, "Seek his face!"
Your face, oh, Lord, I will seek.
Psalm 27:8

31

DRY BONES

THE PROPHET EZEKIEL WAS SHOWN a valley of dry bones and was asked if those bones could live. What would you have answered? He was required to prophesy, to preach the word of the Lord over those dry, dead bones. Parts of our lives can be like dry bones: habitual structures of daily living, seemingly useless unrelated parts of existence, duty and choice, offering no visible condition of profit for the kingdom of our Lord. Are there words or actions in our lives that testify of the power of Jesus to save or to strengthen one in the fight for morality and a good conscience. Once a year, in the lessons about interviews, you allowed the class to interview you, another teacher or another believer. You could hold a Christmas party and use some Scriptures in puzzles; sing Jingle Bells and Silent Night. It was fun for the students, but a slow yet necessary form of witness for the worker who longed for more opportunity. However, it was so limited. Those who spent long years to learn the difficult language were careful not to overstep the bounds and invite loss of job, visa or expulsion. We loved our students and strove to be the best teachers ever; but it meant limitations; we could not speak our minds or hearts about God.

In a country where there is no freedom of proclamation and a history of wars with "Christian" countries, you find few seekers and tough built-in resistance. Even when Turks declare themselves secular, there exists a tradition of antipathy and distrust. In matters of religion, it is even more serious. In a few cases there is a rejection of the past: but only by mistreated minorities such as the Alevi, a Shiite division of Islam, and a few radical Ataturk followers; who take the hero's teachings to its logical extremes. For the others it was a case of show me, don't tell me. Skeptics can only be persuaded by example. The correspondence courses were one of the most effective tools for the introduction of Holy Scripture. A private, yet impersonal, way of one on one communication, it could be shared or hidden and answered shortly or leisurely by the student. One could take months to reply to each lesson or do it in a rush. They could stop any time they pleased. No one else need know. One could take it alone or take it with a friend. They could satisfy their curiosity and see what Christianity is all about. Replies, standardized as they were, offered room for emotional feedback and sharing between student and teacher. With time names become familiar as the lessons proceeded. Personal questions could be asked. Confession or rejection frequently punctuated such correspondence. The encouragement caused by these letters, both individual and numerical, animate many of the workers. However, only a small number of the workers are privileged to share that labor of love.

As foreigners we were easily identifiable, and as such, not always appreciated. You either belong to Islam, dress and act as they do, or you are an easily identified outsider or minority. We tried to wear our label *Yabanje*, foreigner, (derived from the root word wild or savage) with Christian grace and charm. In all things we tried to please. We tried to be friendly every day, while buying bread, riding the bus or shopping; trying to impress an alien culture with our openness and ability to face life in a different manner from that to which they cling so tenaciously. This too, proved dry bones at times. There were long stretches of what seemed profitless routine and always, repeated disappointments. The message was often ignored, misunderstood, rejected, or the contact lost. We would begin again.

Within the church, there were spats, divisions, gossip and narrowness; without, there were politics, blame, envy, false impressions and ignorance. Different congregations were formed to be international in composition and used English and promoted other smaller linguistic groupings: Turkish, Arabic, Farsi (Persian) and Korean meetings. Most were tiny and sometimes drifting; dry bones at best. What could we show for 12 years in this harsh spiritual environment? Very little was visible. Some of the sending societies refused to allow their personnel to be involved with other than Turkish nationals. Others demanded certain levels of language progress within definite time frames or the family was sent home. Unrealistic demands were made by people in home countries who were not exposed to the same environment. Some radicals thought the local people should decide what the church was to be. The new converts were not able to set the norms in the congregation, they were learners. The urge to experiment seemed universal. No one had great success witnessing or interesting middle-eastern people in the Gospel. We felt they needed salvation but how to approach and convince them, seemed to be outside our experience or knowledge. No one knew what, or how to do a more effective job. However, the time was at hand when change would make truth apparent.

One group sent a math professor to teach math in English, but on arrival he decided to plunge into Turkish language study as well. His group was scandalized although he and his wife made amazing progress and had great communication skills within two years. They were musicians and fit into so many situations. They helped form our Asian-side church.

Another slightly older family were given two years to learn the language by another group and when they failed the test shipped them out of the country. He told me sadly, "My father always said I'd fail at anything I attempted." I concluded that the father was not a Christian, but the sending body was supposed to be. It's dry bones to see men fail.

Another man came with family but not connected to any sending body except his church. They had no orientation or preparation for entering the culture. He talked to his wife of going to Mexico, she objected. Later, when he mentioned Brazil:, she asked what was wrong with Mexico. By the time he decided Turkey was the goal, she was wondering about Brazil. He knew you could teach English and get a visa so he came with a Masters degree. He lived over a half hour beyond the nearest workers and spent most of his day and evenings with the job, cramming to prepare the lessons. His beautiful wife was left with the two pre-teen girls and a year old boy at home. They had ample financial support but one does not live by bread alone.

They made many friends in the neighborhood. The girls found some their own age, though it was hard to communicate. One young Libyan man, working as a chauffer, lived nearby and spoke English. He was able to help the parents in getting settled. He became a friend of the family. He helped the husband buy a car and do the paper work for the installation of a telephone. Without a husband most of the day, the wife depended on this man to help her shop, put the girls in a local school, where they understood nothing, and teach her to how cook local foods.

They came to our house church with their new friend and we tried to help and advise them. Ladies made special trips to visit and to help. Families tried to include them in their activities. During several months we could detect changes. If the young friend came with them the girls insisted on sitting in his lap, hanging about his neck and rubbing themselves against him. It was distracting and we spoke to both father and mother about this impropriety, but they said that he was such a dear friend and the girls loved him so. He was, it seemed, necessary for their continuing survival in the country.

Suddenly the marriage began to rupture into arguments, anger and frustrations. Many individuals tried to intercede, but the affair ended in the departure of the wife to be with her lover. When informed, their home church advised their return. Friends took care of the details of house and goods, packing through the night. The girls had a farewell sleepover with friends. Someone watched over the baby. They tried to get in touch with the estranged wife. They found someone who knew where she was. They left the message that they would leave the house at five A.M., she could join them there or at the airport at 7 AM. If she did not appear by boarding time, they would turn her passport over to the police. They would tell them that she had stayed with an illegal immigrant, who had no passport. Finally, the lover told her to go home, he could never marry her and take her home to his family. She arrived at the house at dawn just as they were departing to get the flight. Their friends sadly saw them off.

He phoned me a few days after arrival in his home town for a man to man talk.

He asked if it were possible to return in a few years. I asked him how long it had been after the flight started before they made attempts to reconcile. He said about an hour. I said that was about the time they left Turkish air space and were over Europe. They were out of the war zone by that time. We are engaged in spiritual warfare and the hottest spot at that time was in the east zone where workers were extending their witness. The area they lived in. They were its casualties. These were not the only ones who started well, but finished fruitless. This kind of bone sticks in the throat.

Increasingly, the world was on the move. Ease of travel, rapid wire and radio communications introduced strangers round the world to lands where the grass was greener and the promise of wealth beckoned. Minorities became restive living under local pressure, and politics became deadly in lands of violence. Refugees increased. Transients - Africans, Asians and East Europeans - were stranded all over the middle-east while trying to work their way to western Europe, especially England, France or Germany. Some had Christian backgrounds, but all were under pressure to get food, money, documents and another try at the border crossing. Their plight was pitiful; their stories of hardships they had suffered were convincing. Add to these foreigners, the young people escaping the social bonds of the small village and the family restrictions, to come to the big city "to seek their fortune."

However, the choice had been theirs in many cases. Groups and workers that could, began to spend more time on servicing the needs of the new arrivals. It kept us busy but their behavior did not create a good impression on the local inhabitants. The police were active jailing those caught without proper papers. Newcomers sold smuggled or stolen goods on the street, rushing away at the first sign of police. They begged in the churches and mosques. Buddhist, Muslim, Christian or Communist, they made the rounds. The churches were first, they were known to be merciful. We received letters from rural parents in the country thanking us. One letter said: "Our village is Muslim, yet the only ones to help my son buy the bus ticket back to us, were the Christians. Receive our blessing." Letters of thanks came back from Europe from some who found a refuge there. It was a long hard road through interviews with the United Nations High Commissioners' office, gathering papers and signatures on those. Many had destroyed their passports so that they could not be sent back to their home country. They were escaping poverty, prejudice, dictatorship, religious persecution or Communism.

Workers visited those detained and provided Scriptures. Not one of us knew if it was profitable for the Lord's work, but no one else was interested in helping them, so we had to. The churches and workers got caught up in helping the newcomers, it changed us, but we were too busy to notice. We were serving others, not proclaiming, serving. Not Turks, but needy people and things began to change as the local people watched us. We established clothes depots, food banks, employment files and legal contacts with consulates and police. We really did care for those displaced, unwashed multitudes of poverty-stricken people. Christianity proved its claims and its words were validated. Growth was everywhere apparent in the churches, first with the outsiders; then with the local people. You could feel the difference. The meetings came alive: theory, theology and service became one. We became the body of Christ as any could see.

It was time for us to go home in 1991. We didn't want to, but a deficit was in existence at home and young couples were waiting for support to go and start language study. Marshall calculated that we would have the equivalent of our salary in the funds awaiting us at retirement age. We decided to terminate at that point in time and return on our own initiative to finish what would have been our normal term of service. This would free our salary for someone to start language school sooner. We would do our work without burdening any church economically. We already had prayer support assured through many faithful friends scattered everywhere.

Dry bones were coming together and producing growth in the major cities where workers were located, but a new area in the south-east was sterile. It was another case of dry bones to be cried over and prayed for. Here too, the future looked very unpromising for the gospel. Only God could affect a change in them. We would work there for three years more. In that time we saw the work in Turkey expand and we realized we could not keep up with the in-rush of workers, much less with the work and new believers. A few weeks spaced by years would be the most we could do after 1995.

The question in biblical days was "Can these dry bones live?" Ezekiel saw the answer in chapter 37 of his book. We have lived in the valley of dry bones. Life, out of dead situations, is still a question in many places today. We saw an answering movement start in Turkey; life from bones. We have a God who brings the dead to life.

(At Lazarus' tomb) Jesus wept. Then said the Jews, "Look how he loved him."
John 11:35, 36

Marshall & Hazel Thompson

This is what the Lord says: In the time of my favor I will answer you, and in the day of salvation I will help you; I will keep you...
Isaiah 49:8

32

NEW OPPORTUNITIES

JOHN WAS A MYSTERY TO US: as shifting as water and as unstable, yet full of zeal for the Lord. His wife Selma, on the other hand, was stable, even-tempered and practical. She seemed to incorporate so many virtues and John was still a teenager or even younger in temperament and attitudes. He still attended the church in a casual way but when we returned from home assignment he gladly greeted us as father and mother. We went to eat lunch at his nice little apartment and saw his computer game console after church at the nightclub building. Selma was attending a few classes at university.

The Asian-Side Church met in a rented music hall on Sunday morning after the dancers and drinkers had gone home. We had lots of room, even if it had a strong smell of tobacco and hard drinks. There were about forty of us. It was basically the same group that had started in Tom and Gladys's' front room and transferred to our apartment when the Asian-side group's workers decided to join us. They, in our time of home assignment, had found this public place. It didn't last long, there was a fire in the club and we were forced to move out after only a few months' meetings. The day school for the worker's kids had found a house in a place four stations down the train line, which would serve as school for their Asian-side students. They needed someone to help pay the cost and we made a seven-year agreement that would house our church and serve their students. Volunteer work teams descended on the building, cleaning and modifying the rooms for an auditorium. We got the building ready and dedicated it to God's service and He filled it up. We started getting Turkish language students who wanted their children to be nurtured in

English Church until they all learned Turkish. They wanted to exercise their right to form the church but not to work; not in visitation or any other church duty. They wished to be hearers and formers of policy, but not to contribute anything except money. A few did all the church work, but it was not enough. At this time the school people again tried to legalize the presence of a foreigner's school, but the Turkish Education Department was not interested. After all, no Turkish child attended, no Turkish teacher taught, the courses were designed for children that would continue education in another nation. It was easy for the National Department to shrug and say it was not possible to register it; there was nothing Turkish about any of it and it didn't cost them anything.

We were able to start a Turkish meeting on Sunday afternoons. So a few of us came early to church and stayed late. The church and school functioned about five years before the owners in Germany sold it. So church and school later sought another property near the wharf in Kadikoy.

John would mysteriously appear and disappear periodically. He always had beautiful stories of how he had witnessed to the man who issued visas, to the one who renewed his passport and other brave actions, but we had no way of checking them and we had grown skeptical. His family relations were better; his father came to Istanbul and visited for cancer treatment. Howard and Claudia had them, with us, over for a meal. He moved into a more important job in an appliance store. He complained about the work, but we helped them move to a plush apartment building. They were a happy couple. I asked when they would start having a family. Selma replied, "One child in the family is enough". We knew she meant John.

The next time we returned and visited Istanbul a year later, we learned she had divorced him and married one of her university professors. She had changed her census card back to Muslim in the process.

I spent my last year as a worker copying a translation done by one of my students from Marmara University English classes. She had translated it for Mary who taught the course several times using Gladys's' living room for 12 to 15 learners. I put it on computer in Turkish. I had experience reading my students handwriting and had little trouble. I typed up an Old Testament survey; book one, for computers to print up books, as they were needed. They have been used to teach the study repeatedly since then. We finished out our year and left our apartment in May for a parade of Christian workers, including a film crew to use for the year of our absence. Each small group stayed a month or two, which was a real help for them and for us.

We retired from our board, stored our goods and went back to Turkey after Christmas. We returned to close out the apartment by bringing it into the same condition as when we had contracted it. This involved sanding and polishing the floors. It took some time and effort but we did so and received our original damage deposit. We tried to catch up with the activities of John.

John, the bachelor, now headed the appliance outlet with a dozen people working under him. He assured me that he hired Christians and spoke with some of them of his faith in Christ. He had his chauffeur pick us up to visit his shop. It was beautifully decorated and attended. His personnel liked him and seemed happy on the job. He cultivated a lush life style. He frequented the spots the tabloids cover and he was photographed with the daughters of prominent men. He complained that some fathers phoned him regularly. I asked if he was kissing the girls. He admitted it. "Parents hope for a good marriage for their girls, they wonder what you are up to-- what your motives are toward their daughters. Have you thought of this?" I asked him. He said he meant no harm. We talked conduct and Scripture. But, you never knew what he thought about it. We stayed with him in his apartment while we readied our own rooms for return to the owner.

We sold our phone to a young teacher at what was once Robert's College now a Turkish university. We were moving to Mersin and I would have time to dedicate to writing a Turkish novel and doing local witnessing. We had done the research years before and arranged to leave some of our goods with Hamid, an elementary school teacher. When we were settled near Mersin we set to work.

Sundays we went to Adana for the nearest church an hour away. When we moved to the country we caught two buses to Adana, two hours away for church. The international English church was under great pressure by the local police because they met in a hotel. The Turkish Protestant Church was functioning with a foreign English teacher as it's pastor. There were many problems; including doctrinal differences and what may have been police informants in the congregation.

A Baptist pastor was in charge of the English church while we were there, but he was forced to take a church in Cairo later because of legal interference in the congregation's life.

We were privileged to stay at the Turkish Government's Teachers' Hotel in Mersin, since we had taught at Marmara University. The food was good; the prices on a national level and we were downtown. Young people in Tourist-Hospitality courses at the University ran the hotel. They had to do hands-on work attending the guests. They were interesting contacts. Our friends, Solmaz and Ahmed, parents of one of Mary's young roommates, had arranged the stay. They also rented us their summerhouse in the mountains, but it was early spring. Snow still lingered in a few sheltered spots in the hills. We froze!Though they lent use a small electric heater - we STILL froze! We stuck it out, while the orchard bloomed around us.

There, too, we would write, pray, visit and bear witness to the life in Christ.

Near Mersin were Christian workers with whom we met in prayer for the work. One was preparing sermons to be broadcast from Moscow in Turkish. The new Russia needed capitalist cash to keep the equipment up and personnel paid. Religion was suddenly an acceptable subject for broadcasting especially toward the south in another language. Other friends worked nearby. During this time a South African couple arrived to work and pray. Spring came. It was warm at last, fruit trees bloomed in the mountains. Bouganvilla bloomed near the post office in Mersin and we had to leave until the next year.

We had to spend six months and a day each year in our retirement country to get the old age pension and avoid the charge of abandonment. We now had several jobs to keep up. Besides reporting the work to the interested churches; Marshall was learning French in Summer Courses at a local university. We were writing books and working in a central church while helping in another rural mission for Vacation Bible School. We kept busy. God made it rewarding.

On our second yearly trip to Mersin we left later in the year in March and we waited to go to the mountains. We moved to the seacoast first and spent the month of Ramazan in what would later be a crowded beach resort. We were there alone, I knew we would be watched closely in the town and I had no intention of keeping the fast. We thought there would be less offence if we were out of sight. I had to work on the neglected novel and we had much to occupy us. At the beach, we had only the gatekeeper to contend with. The fact that I kept the fast for three days just in sympathy and to know how others would feel, impressed the gatekeeper and family. They even invited us to one of their sumptous meals, to break the fast after sunset, in good Muslim fashion. Turkish people are always great hosts and their food is delicious and nutritious. We went home after midnight, but did not have to wake up for breakfast before morning light as they would.

We discovered that the Mediterranean Sea is not warm in winter. It is too chill to swim in. Even with unclouded skies and palm trees, the climate is cold. The cold dry wind came sweeping down the mountain range in the early morning, before we got up, so it didn't bother us. When we wrote, we sat in the sunny patio, bundled in a blanket with hats and sunglasses. At 4 PM the wind came back off the water with a vengeance. It was always humid, sharp and cutting. We would take a walk every afternoon to exercise and get warm. but I put on my earmuffs to protect me from the wind, and my big red sun hat on top of it to protect me from the sun. We wore heavy jackets. The beach houses, built to be cool, really are hard to heat. The floors were all tile—no rugs. There was no effort to make windows or doors keep out drafts. At night we huddled before our small butane gas heater to absorb all the warmth possible. The little TV screen two meters away showed what appeared to be ants booting a soccer ball around. Day ended as we heated the water for the hot water bottle, which went first to Hazel's cot. Then we returned to the kitchen to drink some hot milk. We retired to two small cots piled high with covers and coats where Marshall got the hot water bottle, at least for a time. It still took a while to get warm enough to sleep.

The exception was the hot water from the roof solar panels. You could take a hot bath in a cold bathroom. After 3PM on a sunny day the water was hot. However, stepping onto the cold tile floor, you were chilled before you finished drying off.

You had goose pimples after a nice hot bath. No wonder we had the whole forty units to ourselves.

We had rented the seaside cottage from a dentist whose nephew in Istanbul had recommended us. The son, of the same profession, was a charming atheist. The father was an impatient Muslim, who on one visit to us at his place, decided to do his *namaz*, (Muslim worship) in the cottage since it was the proper time. I made no objections. I was sitting on the south side of the room and thought he would face east. Not so! Mecca is southeast over the water. He indicated I was to move. I joined my wife and his on the east and waited for him to finish. I gave him my attention and he soon finished under the admiring smile of his wife. He was witnessing to me. Witnessing is a two way street. Each has to share his view. Duty is the stuff that external religion is made of, but faith is the engine that keeps it running. Without faith, God is not pleased and duty will falter soon after.

We enjoyed a very warm reception in the high mountain village on our second year's visit. The *Imam's* wife visited Hazel and invited us to the parsonage, so to speak, for a meal. We exchanged gifts. Mine was in Turkish; so was his. I gave him a New Testament and he gave me an Explanation of Islam. Both extending the very best we knew; something precious. Both encountering the same community problems: many men do not honor God and debase the morals of the community.

We had the privilege of house holding for a German family in Adana at the end of our second year's return to Mersin. We had gone to the mountains, but Hazel had some back problems that terminated in a doctors examination and a hospital stay on a bed-board for ten days.

I had visited an American friend just before I went to the Doctor. She had shown me the beginning of a crocheted afghan. She had almost finished the squares and all they needed was to be sewn together. I offered to sew them together so I wouldn't be bored to death. She agreed, and I took the pieces home. When the doctor ordered me to bed. I Instructed Marshall to bring the whole bag full of pieces to me to finish in the hospital.

The Doctor protested that I was to remain flat on my back. So I showed him that I could be flat on my back and still crochet. He had offered a TV, but I explained that I would be much happier doing the handwork for my friend. He was very helpful to us and we developed an appreciation for him.

Marshall went back to move our stuff out of the mountain house, to return it to Ahmed bey. He said good-bye to the *Imam* and his assistant, our neighbors, and their families. The handsome young son of the assistant was called *Isa*, Jesus, and was newly married to a beautiful young bride. It is in these country people that one sees the best of the simple and good in Turkey. The *Imam* came to the van that served the village for mobility to the city. He was a young man so we held hands as we walked, the way fathers and sons do in their society. I said *Elveda* the definite farewell, meaning "I probably won't see you again". Uprightness exists in individuals of other societies and religions. However, the knowledge of God becomes personal and complete only through Christ's salvation.

We spent the remainder of that time with the Adana people, who were still trying to work out their church and state relations. Hazel required extra attention and care. I gave away much of our stored goods to the local people and charities before we left to take up our "six months and one day" life at home. We visited our children and grandchildren scattered through out the United States.

The gospel work of the churches was in a process of expansion. Workers and believers were in many of the towns, where before, there had been only the report of one or another believer, isolated and secretive. Now some of our friends from Istanbul were in those small towns working as teachers and shepherding small house churches. After we were retired our finances made possible the practice of visiting them every spring and encouraging them in the work. Circumstances were always contrary for the workers, but imperceptibly the work was growing over time. Our arrivals and departures were always by way of Istanbul. We loved the place and the people too much to go home and forget them.

When your aim is to help others achieve some desired end, you become part of a process that integrates you into their society. Turks wanted our language and our encouragement as they accepted our technology and commerce. We were glad to give that and with our friendship those values which are most important to us. All men are justly proud of the values that they see as most important in the development and progress of their lives. Our friends taught us their values and we gave them ours, without apology. We all profited and none felt put upon. Most honored Jesus and did not find it strange that we did too. The test question was that to associate Him with God; Emanuel, God with us, was for some, *shirk:* polytheism.

*For my thoughts are not your thoughts,
neither are your ways my ways;
declares the Lord.*
Isaiah 55:8

33

TRYING TO SET THINGS RIGHT

MUCH CAN HAPPEN IN A country when you are absent nine months. We never did spend a full year home when we worked in Turkey. It seemed more happened, there were more changes in Turkey, even the name, every time we went home. The rate of inflation and devaluation of money changed every time we returned to Istanbul. Prices and politics were always different.

Before we left Istanbul on our third visit after retirement, we acquired the task of putting the second book of the Old Testament Survey on computer for Bible instruction. Marshall did this on his laptop computer while in Adana. We were staying with one of the lady workers whose partner had moved. She had been left with the whole apartment to pay for. We moved in to help her make payment and to spend this third visit in Adana where both the English and Turkish services had been prohibited or destroyed. New understandings with government and between Christians needed to be forged.

The place of women in the congregation had become an issue. It had to be worked over and the meetings started again. The presence of many denominations complicated the matter among the workers. We started having what Marshall called Friend's meetings. Communion was a coffee and sweet roll after service. No one taught the Scripture, but even women could tell what they understood and how it affected them subjectively. This did not consist of "women taking authority over men" or teaching. One young man objected to a woman leading music, even if a man picked out the hymns. He wanted women to pray in a separate group when we broke up for minute prayers. There were enough people who felt this way that we did not wish to offend them, they on the other hand had to give up some things. English and Turkish services limped along. Still Adana was once the place where workers were killed or died in the sixties and seventies. Then it became the place that arrested and expelled workers in the eighties and nineties. The expulsion of two young men, one Swedish the other Korean, the year before had brought a new wave of workers, some veterans from other areas to the Adana region. It had become a place where the opposition was both local and grudging as well as national and governmental. The spiritual ambient had shifted and the traditions were giving way ever so slowly. St. Paul never mentions a church in Tarsus, his home region. It has evidently always been tough.

While we were there, Annie (who shared her apartment with us) often visited Filiz, a young businesswoman who ran a brides' shop. She was the breadwinner in her household. Her two brothers were both baptized believers. Annie was always a welcome guest in their home. They prayed for the salvation: of their sister, parents and extended family. Filiz and her mother attended services regularly, but had never made public commitments. One brother had married one of the Christian workers, and they were in the States studying so that he could become a pastor. Other young men of the church envied him. The younger brother was just back from his military service and looking for a job.

Annie was in the midst of an exam period where she was teaching English, so was terribly busy when she received a call one Thursday evening. It was quite late when she arrived home. She had papers to grade and tests to prepare, so she thought she would wait until after the Saturday morning classes, when her duties would relax a little, to call back. All day Friday they played phone tag with no contact. However, she got another call from them during school hours Saturday. They were desperate and asked if she could come and sit with Filiz so the family members would be free to go home and get some rest. Nursing shortages were such in the hospital that they kept someone present twenty-four hours a day to watch over the loved one.

Feliz had felt a little bad Thursday afternoon, so they took her to the Doctor, who immediately put her in the hospital. By 4PM Friday, they were telling the family they hadn't determined what it was, but that it was serious enough that they might lose her. Annie called from school and asked us to put some of the kitchen leftovers into a bowl that she could take with her when she dropped by the house to leave her books. She would eat it in the hospital room. We did as she asked, and she barely took time to change and hurried away. We took time to pray, however, that she would have the opportunity to lead the lady to the Lord. Upon arrival at the hospital, she found that several people who were suffering from the same virus infection had already died, and that Filiz was in a coma.

Annie came home around 9AM Sunday, after her friend had slipped away in the early morning hours. Filiz had never regained consciousness, while Annie had kept that lonely vigil. We had fixed her some breakfast while she bathed, had a short rest and was off again to help the family prepare for the interment.

Contacting the son in the United States was a problem. The couple had spent some months in Oregon, but was headed for a Bible School in the east of that country, where he would study and she would work in the office. They had piled all their worldly goods into the car and had started east the day before. When the Turkish call came to her parents about the death, they didn't know how they could get in touch with the couple. An hour after the sad news came, they had a call from their daughter. The car had broken down somewhere in Montana, they had put it into the garage, and found a place to stay, planning to be there until it could be fixed. When they got the news; they arranged about the car, went to the nearest big center, bought a ticket for Turkey, and flew. They arrived Monday afternoon.

We didn't get to church that morning. Annie had been exposed to this virus; she exposed us. There were several families with young children who attended and they asked that we not come, lest we bring in the germs. They had determined at the hospital that it was a particularly vicious strain of meningitis.

Though the boys were both believers, the parents were not. The father was very indifferent, and the mother just didn't seem to understand. Annie continued to spend the moments she could with the family, and heard the mother telling the neighbors of her experience.

It seems that while the daughter was ill, the mother had had a dream. When the people came to do the "mourning" she said that they shouldn't worry about her daughter. In her dream Filiz was dressed in one of her beautiful wedding gowns. The Lord Jesus came to take her away to heaven. The mother declared that when she died, that she was also going to go and be with Filiz and the Lord Jesus, too. When they heard it, one of the neighbors revealed that she, too, had had a similar dream. That Filiz was dressed in a wedding dress, and was borne away to heaven by Jesus. When the son arrived with his Christian worker wife, she was able to help them confirm their commitment to the Lord.

The Turkish Protestant Church came together at her funeral and there were signs of sorrow and reconciliation among some. However, the church did not come back together as a meeting or fellowship.

One of the believers who worked at the American Air Base was from the disrupted and scattered Turkish church. He made us his particular interest. He blamed the disruption on the foreign pastor and teacher, who had refused to help him. He affirmed that although local security forces had harassed him, no one in the church would believe him. I tended to believe that he was threatened with the loss of his job at the U.S. base if he didn't cooperate with internal security. He was intent on learning who the new workers were and where they lived. He was convinced they were all spies. We tried to arrange for reconciliation with the teacher now working in another large city. We had phone calls and a local man in the other city offered mediation. Neither seemed enthusiastic. Eventually they met and things seemed to get better for a while, but he seemed psychotic in his fears and anger. When he learned from other sources where someone lived he would grill us about it. I told him it was none of his business since these people did not intend to work with his group. He felt he had a right to know and that they were up to no good purposes. I told him the *Kaymakam*, an official of a district of a city or suburb, and the local housing authority, knew where every foreigner in the city lived. He could clear with them if he was worried. He would get very emotional and say we didn't trust him. He was right. He knew I was revising a book and would be leaving after a few months. He seemed to feel the need to have his doubts refuted. I felt he was a believer who had to satisfy police or internal security with information about Protestant activities. They harassed him. I felt sorry for him. After all the authorities were in a position to get their own data.

There was only one set of printed sheets of the second book of Old Testament Survey. It was the sequel to the one I had put on computer four years before. Someone else had put this one on computer and printed the proofs. Then, at a later date the computer and disk had gotten a virus that destroyed the original. It lacked back translation and a new disk to print from. I had volunteered to do this bit of work. Working in Turkish, I got it all copied and in usable form by the time our three-month visit was up. While we were in Adana we saw the new workers and friends, who transferred from another part of the country, start a new work and the basis seemed more balanced. Annie moved back to the Istanbul area a year later. We found that our group was concentrating their resources on teaching Scripture. The presence of foreign teachers in the university work was closing down because of budgetary limits of the Turkish government. Their funding was concentrating on using more national teachers. Bad experiences with foreign personnel limited the hiring of outsiders. Disgruntled Western teachers had sued the government because of contract violations. The university's situation was temporarily a mess. God was turning new pages for the workers. Customary channels were clogged, but new opportunities were opening doors everywhere.

After a three months stay in the south of Turkey, we visited John on the way back through Istanbul. We left him some pictures and books we hadn't room to take. He promised to send them to us by mail. He told us of going back to Iran and that he was getting a new passport locally and witnessing to the consul. We prayed with him and left. He was going to take us to the airport on our departure. We returned to stay the night with Howard and Claudia. We talked to him on the phone. He was very busy, but insisted that he would take us to the airport. He never showed up! At 4 o'clock in the morning I had to run out and get a taxi! We never saw him again and the books and pictures never arrived. When Marshall returned nine months later others occupied the apartment and he had lost his job as manager.

We wondered if his reconciled father had died of cancer. John might have returned to Iran. We heard many stories: "He was in prison"; "He was martyred"; "He had renounced the faith"; "He was living in sin"; "He was hiding somewhere in Turkey." We never had any rumor confirmed. Successive visits to the city did not help. Some people heard others say they had seen him in the city. Other folks thought he had remained in Iran. Newer people didn't even know him. He remains a mystery, but I still pray for him. The book of Hebrews, chapter 11, tells us there is a cloud of witnesses in heaven. They see all the secret and hidden things that people do. Some day we'll know all about it.

*My eyes will be on the faithful in the land,
that they may dwell with me.*
Psalm 101:6

34

THE TALE ENDS

INSTEAD OF RETURNING TO TURKEY in 1995 as we had the previous three years for a three months visit, we answered God's calling in a different way. In July Hazel went on a volunteer work project in Bolivia and then to Argentina for the Baptist World Alliance Congress in Buenos Aires. At the same time Marshall launched himself on a long dreamed of visit to three trouble spots of the World: Ulster in Northern Ireland, Israel and the South African Republic. He spent three weeks in each area to see the condition of the three lands of bitter, long lasting conflicts and their Christian minorities. Which country would resolve their differences and which could not?

Ulster was a case of invasion and occupation, for over five centuries it had been going on. Colonization is always a violent affair and the occupation of another tribe's lands leads to bitter struggles, even up to our present age. Differences of language, religion, race and culture always mark and mar such clashes. In the Irish case the language was lost, the culture modified, the race with little to no differences and both claiming to be different kinds of Christians. Surely this claim would bring some kind of understanding and settlement. Christians are called to love one another. Would peace come?

I had been led by internal questionings into a study of the Jubilee (Leviticus 25:11). Moses declared that every 50 years Israel should return assigned family lands to the original owners. Capitalization of the dispossessed is an appealing idea. The first Jubilee for modern Israel could come as a blessing to the world. The logical opportunity should happen near the year 1998; fifty years after independence. The God of Israel had proclaimed the festival to secure the distribution of wealth necessary to keep the land free and in the hand of farming freemen. Alienated lands would be returned to the original families. Loyalty to one's people would be insured by economic opportunity. Hope for a better future lay in sight for each generation. What a father or grandfather had lost or sold could be regained by son or grandson. Strong stable family ties and traditions would result. Would Israel catch this vision? Was loyalty to Moses real?

South Africa was another land of violence and divisions. A long struggle had culminated in a change of government from a white racial minority to a majority of less educated, less fiscally secure people with diverse cultural backgrounds and languages. Would harmony or discrimination result from the changes of structures and rulers? Would ethnic cleansing result? What would happen to Indian, mixed Coloreds and tribal minorities? Could the growing crime wave be controlled?

Marshall had been researching these matters and was ready to enter the arena to bear witness to God's ability to save countries as well as individuals. The experience was unforgettable.

Marshall returned to Turkey a year later, for a month, in the fall of 1996. Jay, his original host there, was now working for the Zwimer institute and was conducting on site orientations in Turkey for people planning to do gospel work in what used to be Soviet Turkistan. Marshall functioned as a resource person and was able to add personal anecdotes to the orientation lectures. He was very busy as he can tell you.

I visited the people and institutions I knew, where I had participated in the gospel witness. I stayed with Roc and Cap again and got to know Doc and Jan, volunteer psychologists serving for what became two, two year terms. They trained others and taught courses. I sat in on some of the courses they were putting on tape and helped in the filming of one segment. They were going to take a vacation later and I helped with visa and other footwork. Our friend Turkhan had married again and was leading a church with success, His daughter, Kami, was growing up. Change was everywhere evident. The Asian-side Church had suffered a major disruption and was starting over with a smaller body of workers. Koreans were a growing presence. There was a Korean church and their workers attended many of the Turkish or English congregations.

I was able to get a local Istanbul to Israel ticket within budget and so spent a month in Jerusalem gardening for St. Paul's church and also at the Garden Tomb while visiting most of the country. I followed up contacts from the year before, trying to convince them of the importance of the Jubilee that God proclaimed through Moses. Two years were lacking for the first Jubilee date for Israel: 1998 would be the fiftieth year from Independence. Church growth was notable everywhere in both Israel and Turkey. The school for workers' children in Istanbul grew in size and scope.

Again, in 1997, I returned to Istanbul to serve as a resource person for Jay and Kay teaching at a house rented by the Zwemer institute. I was able to procure a visa to Uzbekistan, from the consulate in Istanbul, which I had been unable to do in North America. Our host family, Ahmed, Solmaz and children from Mersin had come to Istanbul to see a doctor about the deafness developing in one daughter. We met for prayer and catching up on our lives. Again, I visited friends and churches for a month. I got caught up on the news and noted the advances. This visit produced unexpected moments that changed my life in a marked way.

The first day in Istanbul traveling from the airport to Doc's house I lost (perhaps had stolen?) part of my Traveler's checks! They were in a small nylon travel bag. In it were ten checks of one hundred dollars each. I did not notice it immediately, I had large luggage to attend to. After the discovery in the Doc's house I called the checks' banking headquarters in London and Hazel who also called around for me. I had enough cash to take care of the immediate needs. However, at the local bank the agent who refunded the lost checks had only one thousand denomination left! No fifties, hundreds or even five hundreds could be had. I got a one thousand US$ check. Fortunately I had five Canadian one hundred-dollar checks in a suitcase that was not lost. However in a country where money devaluates daily you don't want to change large amounts into cash. You lose too much on the transitions. Turkey was suffering galloping inflation, so I eked out changing the Canadian checks as needed. I discovered the new banking ATM machines would yield money on my bankcard. To think of all the tears and troubles we wasted on money exchange before. Travel is now much easier, I mistakenly, thought. At times optimism can be the prelude to disaster.

I was able to house sit and bridge Doc's departure and the arrival of Tom and Gladys, who would replace them temporarily. They kept the accounts, holding the house until Doc and Jan's return after a medical visit home. I left a few days after Tom's arrival.

I flew on to Uzbekistan where in Tashkent I was able to find banking services for the Canadian checks and get the required train ticket to visit Kokand and the Fergana Valley, where one of my stories is set. I was repeatedly taken for a Russian trying to speak accented Uzbeki and addressed in the Soviet language, Russian, instead of Turkish which I did speak. Uzbekis who listened understood the related dialect of Turkish, but most folks didn't listen long enough to understand.

There was an amazing freedom in the country then under transition. Bibles, Uzbeki and Russian, were sold on the street at the second hand displays spread near the sidewalks. Coming from an atheist past most of the people seemed uncommitted personally. Islamic Missionaries were present and active, but churches were also.

In Uzbekistan the banking problem increased as the local government refused to repurchase their own money for western currency. I exchanged enough to pay the hotel and train ticket to Kokand. I stayed for a week and moved on to Samarkand by bus. There I discovered that they refused to change traveler's checks. They would only take cash. I had twenty-one dollars American. The twenty brought me enough to buy a bus ticket back to Tashkent the next morning. I canceled plans to visit Bukara. So I finished the day viewing the parks, museums, and splendid historic buildings and packed late that night for an early departure. The trip by bus lasted many hours and I thought I would not get to the exchange bank in Tashkent before it closed. I skinned in on the subway just before five and got my last Canadian travelers check cashed. The tourist hotel recommended was much more expensive than I had been told. After a meager meal downtown, I asked the price of the airport ride at the taxi stand. I learned my money would be insufficient. I prayed and decided I would take the first taxi available at the gate next morning. I asked in Russian the price to the airport and the answer was half the amount quoted the night before. As I concluded my boarding procedure. I was informed the exit visa cost ten US. dollars. I had that much in native currency but they insisted on foreign cash. I did not have it. No one would exchange my Rubles for any currency!

An oil geologist loaned me the money. (I invited him, a year later, for a dinner out in Houston Texas. I offered him the ten in cash but he said I must pay him with a copy of my book.) I had nearly ten dollars of Uzbeki rubles left and a one-dollar bill. No moneychanger in the world would give me face value even in the country itself. I gave all of it and bought a two-liter container of orange juice for the long wait in the Istanbul airport. There I noticed that the juice container's country of origin was Israel, the country to which I was in transit. In Israel the same container was worth two dollars.

In Israel, a country with a free market, I changed my one and only thousand dollar US. Traveler's check and was able to trade Shekels back to dollars at the end of the visit. Again I worked on two gardens and visited important biblical sites as well as talk about Jubilee. I stayed in Arab hostels and ate their food and took their tours.

In the Jubilee year of 1998 Hazel went with me to Israel. I told her that if Gog and Magog were due to arrive, as one self-appointed prophet had told me the year before, she wouldn't want to miss it. Fortunately, the invasion didn't coincide. Although the Jewish people ignored Jubilee opportunities, we had a wonderful visit. Hazel was able to climb the two-hour ascent to Masada with me. We enjoyed the sites of the Holy Land and visits to people we had known in Turkey. Opportunities to witness were frequent and Christian fellowship was very satisfying. I gave some seeds to plant at the Garden Tomb as we left. Hazel was disappointed not to visit Turkey as well.

I got the news that fall at home by e-mail and it surprised me. Peter C. Wagner, whom I knew in Bolivia, was sponsoring a Gospel celebration in the Ephesus amphitheater, a Korean Choir and celebrants from around the earth would be present the fifth of October 1999. Knowing Peter, now a professor at Fuller Seminary in southern California, I knew it would be a charismatic and noisy, but well planned and ordered presentation. How his organization got permission through the government I'll never know, but I suspect it was through the tourist division, since it would be conducted in English and was not considered an attempt to convert Turks. I decided I would go directly from Istanbul overnight through Izmir to Seljuk by bus and be there the next morning to join in the celebration. It could be the largest Gospel celebration since the Turkish Republic's founding. I changed my plans and advised my contacts in Turkey of what I should be doing.

Meanwhile, Hazel was needed in Kansas to help our older daughter move. She left at the end of September and was staying until I joined her there for Christmas. Grandchildren expected our visits.

Problems became apparent when I attempted to change my flights, I had problems getting the flight I needed to get there early and ended by accepting a flight the day before the big event. Every thing would have to mesh like clockwork, but it didn't. A tremendous thunderstorm delayed my departure from Moncton, New Brunswick and I missed my flight from Montreal. I took an alternate flight to Toronto to make up time but after a rush through the London airport I got a flight that took me to Istanbul the evening of the celebration. They lost my luggage. I rushed to Mary's apartment buying a change of underclothes from a street front store. I showered, dressed and was served a supper. I left within the hour on the bus to Seljuk. I prayed as the night came and the meeting ended. I got there early the next morning, one day late. I can, at least, say I prayed it through.

I spent a week in Seljuk (Ephesus), city of museums and met some of the people attracted to the celebration. I met youth and pastors from over Turkey and some from Middle Asia training to serve. I visited well-known biblical sites and the now empty stadium where celebrants, some days before, shouted, "Great is Jesus the Messiah". It is the same amphitheater where people once shouted in Paul's day for the glory of the now forgotten goddess Diana/Artemis. The school of Tyrannus is there; the church of St. John and a Crusader Castle also.

October 1999 was just two months after the earthquake that destroyed much of the industrial belt just to the east of Istanbul. When I visited, people were winterizing their tents and building temporary structures. Schools struggled on in tents and plywood box structures. Electricity, water and fuel were spotty and unsure. Many of the people were traumatized and refused to sleep in buildings that were declared safe. I stayed two weeks near Kartal a halfway point with Ron and Catherine, friends from the West.

Aside from meeting the people and visiting the centers for emergency care contributed from abroad and distributed locally, I ventured out on some trips of my own. First to seek an old friend, a Turkish English teacher who lived in one of the destroyed areas. I took the ferry to visit Yalova. There I found his house destroyed in part. It was condemned and no one was allowed to live in it. Some of the neighbors, living in hastily built reinforced tents, gave me information about my absent friend. Mustafa was visiting his hometown when the earthquake happened. He came to see the damage and returned to his home in the east. So I used my day excursion to discover he was alive, but I didn't see him. I took the last boat back and enjoyed the cool two-hour trip. I returned to Istanbul to do further visits and especially to see the progress of Baptist work in the church center near a principal avenue. There were other exciting projects on the Asian side. The church near the wharf was still functional and the mix of workers was greater than ever.

My friend Turkhan was now a recognized minister, co-operating with the Koreans, he had a full church. He wanted a scapula to wear in service with the Jerusalem cross on the two ends. I promised him one from Israel. I knew I would return via the airport on my way home. I actually had a day and using my bankcard at the airport, withdrew the smallest possible exchange. I got one five million-lira bill for about $14.00 Canadian or near ten dollars American. After becoming an instant millionaire I spent half a million on bus fare into Taksim Square. I stayed with a friend whose grandson promised to deliver the package for Turkhan and letters to others. I left him a million for bus and ferry fare. I promised to keep in touch by e-mail. Even after a gift to the household, I still had the bus fare to the airport.

It was my last visit to Turkey. I said a final farewell. I wonder if I will ever see it again. But I am sure of one thing: my prayers for their good, and the proclamation of the Gospel among them, will always be there. In time all these prayers, in Jesus name, will be answered. "Lord, make it so.

Look, the Lamb of God, who takes away the sin of the world!
John 1:29b

35

PINFEATHERS

<u>Pinfeathers</u> – feathers not fully developed.-
Webster's Dictionary

CHANGES IN TURKISH LIFE AND culture came fast at the beginning of the 21th century and technology was changing the face of the people and country.

We arrived at a much improved and larger Ataturk Airport to be met by David Phillips, former executive secretary of the Canadian board, and now overseas worker for that organization. He had greetings and a key card, not to the city, but to the bus, rail, tram, trolley subway and ferry service in the city. All were electronically controlled so that each fare was recorded and deducted from the key card when you insert it into the fare box. It could be reloaded with more TL. (Turkish Lira) worth of travel at a wicket near a dock on the Bosphorus. It was useful for any area of the city.

However, we did not take the subway or boats instead we took a taxi. There you would have to pay the fare in cash. We arrived a half hour later after crossing the bridge between Europe and Asia and several mistaken turns as the driver strove to find Anadolu Sitesi. We drove past the security guard to stop before one of several large apartment complexes where old friends Mike and Deanna lived. David continued with the taxi to his own house which we visited later. The street started at the end of the bus line, and wound upward and around like a conch shell.

We were ordered to bed to nap in anticipation of the arrival that night of several friends among which would be a few names or faces that we remembered.

The talk at dinner was about a serious earthquake followed by several days of tremors that had everyone traumatized when we were living there.

On the eastern outskirts of Istanbul, and the nearby towns, huge apartment buildings had collapsed and had been declared by the government not fit to live in. The police prohibited people from going into many of the apartments because there was so much damage. They thought them so shaky that they might fall. Some sneaked in under cover of darkness to collect a few pieces of clothing and personal treasures, and then fled back to their home towns in the interior that they had come from. We remembered looking for some of our old friends and were not being able to find them.

The government sent in the army to work with all their equipment and personnel to dig out the survivors. Clinics were set up and emergency workers came from all over Turkey, and many foreign countries. They also sent food, medical supplies, and tents to house those whose homes were destroyed.

Trained dogs were brought in to sniff out bodies dead and alive. They detected someone. It was a nurse who had been trapped in the basement of a collapsed building for nine days. She was pinned down, and had no access to food for that whole period. All who could were glued to their televisions to witness the rescues and many were praying for her. Ihey had to exercise extreme caution to keep more beams and pillars from falling in on her. It took a whole day to clear a way to free her.

Teams from local churches volunteered to distribute relief items. Friendships formed at that time became bases for later help to the needy. Trauma teams were formed to speak to groups of neighbors about confidence to trust God first and then neighbors and helpers. Trust is of great value in overcoming fear. Trust in Jesus promotes health and confident living. Perfect love casts out fear. This became so for many of those who had suffered losses. Ynfortunately, Turkey contains four frature zones. When the earth shifts Turks will know it.

On our first Sunday we went to a church where an old friend was acting pastor. There we met an former student from Marshall's English classes at Marmara University. Mi-ne was married to the pastor and become a lawyer in the area of Civil and Religious Rights. We wanted to take them to lunch but they told us of an important marriage to be celebrated in Gedik Pasha Armenian Church in less than an hour. We hurried over in Ron's car. It was difficult to find a parking place. We walked quite a long way from there to the church. The sanctuary was packed out and they took us to the side, left wing seating. We saw many friends as we passed to enter the remaining seats away up front. A Pastors' little daughter, now grown up married a young seminary graduate stood below us. Children grow up and marry. Were we really that old? We met many of those whom we remembered during the reception lunch afterwards. This was to be our most important day on a two week visit. The old days of strife and anguish had passed. Stability and growth had replaced clashes and disasters. By faith and work, prosperity had returned.

We enjoyed some tourist activities and visited Emirgan Park at Tulip time. Hazel and Mike took many pictures, but she lost the CD that contained them.

Marshall made a quick trip to Eritrea for a prayer walk. An erupting volcano in Iceland that interrupted travel all over Europe, almost cut off his return from Eritrea. However, Marshall got an early flight from Cairo back to Istanbul. It was an excuse for another trip to Emirgan Park for our farewell to a country changing rapidly.

Ataturk's secularism lives on in the cities, but the return to political Islam was welcomed in the villages. For the moment variations, even indifference, was tolerated. In a bus load of passengers the women might all be 'covered' (wear Islamic garb),. However, on the street or on a bus, we can see women dressed from the latest Paris fashions mixed with girls in jeans. All are dressed to suit themselves.

Look, I make all things new...
Revelation 21:5

"Children, Have you caught any fish ?"
"No," they answered.
"Cast your net on the right side
of the boat to find some."
John 21:5

36

RENEWEL

'My son, Borden and I arrived from Israel on Turkish Airlines in May of 2014. We landed at what was for me, a totally new airport on the Asian side of Istanbul. It was ample and efficient and we continued our flight to Adana on Pegasus, a new economy airline. The Adana Airport also reflected the booming economy of the Turkish state. The taxi ride to the hotel was effective in spite of the fact that Turkish traffic remains hectic and rapid. Our driver suffered a fender-bender on the way to the hotel and we worried a fight might break out, but lacking significant damage, the drivers settled for an exchange of strong words and went on their ways.

We came two days ahead of our conference to rest. We took a leisurely walk and enjoyed some fresh orange juice. We relished a leisurely meal at the hotel restaurant. Borden e-mailed our arrival to the family and we relaxed and slept.

On Sunday we found the church two blocks from our hotel. It held about sixty worshipers and was led by a pastor from Latin America. The Turkish majority was enthusiastic and prolonged the meeting. Afterwards, we ate in a nice restaurant on the terrace across the street. Why dine inside in May?

Gradually conferees arrived: representatives from America, Brazil, Canada, Europe and Asia gathered to meet and confer at the small church. Our meetings were on the second floor of a large office building near the plaza. Twenty years before, during our previous stay near Adana, there had been one disintegrating church in the city. There were now two gospel Churches in Adana composed of Turkish youth and we visitors were warmly welcomed.

Reports were received of Gospel achievements in Central Asia and the Middle East. Two organizations were merging their ministries: TWO: Turkish World Outreach, that offered Turkish Correspondence courses in the New Testament. It was advertised in newspapers and letters. Crossover was assisting existing congregations by sponsoring of evangelistic outreach in new locations.

Crossover would use the correspondence courses to win new converts. They were combining their special activities. Three days of business were combined with tourism and prayer. The tourism involved historic sights, as well as a new government-built million-dollar mosque, where visitors were welcomed even during worship time.

A bit of exposed Roman Road was viewed in mid town among large office buildings. It was uncovered recently where a large office building was being erected. The Antiquities Department confiscated the property to investigate and explore the site.

We ate lunch at a restaurant located among the rushing rapids of a large stream. Conversation was made all but impossible by the roar of the waters. The place was so crowded that they were hard put to find seating for our party. Naturally, fish was the main menu item.

We visited St. Paul's well and Cleopatra's gate in Tarsus. There were tourist buses everywhere we went. We visited a restored Byzantine church-museum and sang several Gospel hymns while seated in the sanctuary, It turned out to be a splendid photo op.

On Thursday we went on a chartered bus that took us through the Cilician Gates, toward The Plateau, to enjoy our visit to Goromey, and the Underground Cities.

Goromey is a tourist center in a valley full of fantastic formations eroded into the red clay and lime stone of Turkey's central plain. They say that the ancient inhabitants lived on and cultivated the plains. When harvest time came, sometimes the invader came, too. They came to steal the harvested crops. The produce was stored in underground cities where defense was easy. When the invader came, the people took their livestock and went into hiding.

At the entryway there was a large chamber carved out of the rock, and many passages led away from it. When they were hiding they made it look like they were escaping from one of those openings by dropping a little trace of straw across the floor that led out of that big room. It led about a meter, and then turned to the left. Any light they were carrying would not show them that when they turned the corner, they would step into a hole to their death. They have dropped a 3 kilometer- long sounding measure and never touched the bottom.

When we visited these caverns, we enjoyed our dinner in a large room that accommodated our party of a whole bus load. A harpist sat in the vestibule playing soothing music, at the axis of about 4 or 5 chambers where other groups were also being served. Next we went to see the Turkish rugs. There were several young men who in turn unfurled the rugs in the hope of selling to the visitors. I was not interested, since we brought home ours that we bought and used in Turkey when we lived there.

The valley had clay, so there were many potters with every kind of vessel, bowl, vase, cup, plate, figurine or other item imaginable for sale. They demonstrated the use of the potter's wheel, which reminded Borden and me of the Biblical example of God being the potter and we, the clay.

We left in the afternoon for a short flight to Ataturk Airport in Istanbul. Our hotel was on a side street near the Gran Bazaar, across from Istanbul University.

Borden and I used the evening to seek out the old Armenian Church at Gedik Pasha to learn if there would be a service in English on Sunday morning. The church has various ethnic and language meetings during the weekends. They had a special speaker listed and we resolved to go Sunday.

We had our last meeting in a conference room at the hotel. Saturday night after a day of sight-seeing at the Topkapa Palace, the museum and the Hagia Sophia Museum. They are a magnificent sight even with dozens of tour groups pressing around your group speaking Arabic, Chinese, French, German, Japanese, Portuguese, Russian, Spanish, and more. The world presses in to Istanbul to see Emperor Justinian's architectural marvel, a domed building larger than a football field with restored Biblical mosaics gloryfying Jesus. Thousands of people pass through its doors every day. Long lines of groups with guides and electronic audio and cameras pass on endlessly. We had Turkish Christians as guides for the English speakers in our group and the Brazilians had a Missionary for Portuguese. Late Saturday night we had our last meeting and terminated our Conference. Mr.Hagerman could now retire with the knowledge that the work he had begun would be continued by Crossover as a part of their church planting organization. All the areas of the expanding net of churches were reported with goals and problems explained. God's kingdom was continuing its growth and new people and cultures were entering in to the pilgrim mode. Our destination is not here and now, but lies in the future and beyond any human imagination. Mountains will continue to be move! We bonded with each other. Some of us would never meet again in this world, but we expected to see one another again. It sounds strange to say it, but we were family now and forever. I gave out some free e-book computer tickets and some said they would always remember this occasion. I believed them. We retired, but others continued to party and others started the journey home. All thought the nine days well spent.

We attended a service at the Gedik Pasha Armenian Church to hear an electrifying sermon in English and Turkish. Various congregations continue to share the use of the beautiful old building. Sunday evening we explored the use of the subway to make our way to the airport early Monday.

Back at the hotel, we saw some of the remaining conferees off to the airport.

We made several attempts to contact our friend Jon. He had invited us to meet him at his home in Istanbul. However, when we talked to him that Sunday evening, he told us he was leaving Italy on Monday to come home to Istanbul. I realized Jon's character had not changed. We enjoyed the conversation and the exchange of sincere affection, and hope for a future opportunity.

We enjoyed a leisurely breakfast the next morning of Turkish tea and bread with butter and honey, white goat cheese, and black olives.

We departed from the Ataturk Airport on the European part of the city. I mused as we left on the radical changes from the time I visited and lived in these cities. The return of stability had its price tag in exposure to world events and opinions. Limited freedom and recovery of confidence was apparent. The youth looked and dressed like everyone else in the world. Religious freedom seemed to be more possible not only because of secularism in the city, but also the admiration of tourists.

The secular world seemed familiar to villagers. Many had only heard about Europeans and Americans but had never met one. Our friendly Brazilian visitors enchanted everyone. The areas of heavy tourism are the areas most open to the gospel. At last they are accepting a world of infinite variety and are willing to live with it. The struggle for *Tanra*: God, was now to be personal and internal in everyone.

Jesus said: "If you have faith the size of a mustard seed, you will say to this mountain, 'move from here to there' and it will move."

Matthew 17:20

Behold, I stand at the door and knock, if anyone hears my voice and opens the door, I will come in to him and eat with him...

Revelation 3:20

There are many other things which Jesus did...
which are not written in this book.

John 21:25, 26

Printed in the United States
By Bookmasters